The ABC's of HYDROPONICS

Margot Schubert &
Wolfgang Blaicher

Sterling Publishing Co. Inc. New York
Distributed in the U.K. by Blandford Press

Translated by Sigrid Shreeve

Copyright © 1984 by Sterling
Publishing Co., Inc.
Two Park Avenue, New York, N.Y.
10016

Original edition published in
West Germany
under the title
"1 × 1 DER HYDROKULTUR"
© 1981 by BLV Verlags-
gesellschaft mbH, Munich, 1983

Distributed in Australia by Oak Tree
Press Co., Ltd.
P.O. Box K514 Haymarket,
Sydney 2000, N.S.W.

Distributed in the United Kingdom by
Blandford Press
Link House, West Street, Poole,
Dorset BH15 1LL, England

Distributed in Canada by Oak Tree
Press Ltd.
c/o Canadian Manda Group,
P.O. Box 920, Station U
Toronto, Ontario, Canada M8Z 5P9

Manufactured in West Germany

Library of Congress Catalog
Card No.: 84-50579
Sterling ISBN 0-8069-7868-6 Paper

Picture page 2
This VIESSMANN container
('plantell-verto' RECHTECK 100)
and the *Pandanus utilis* is an
impressive decoration for any room.
The false palm, with its enormous
green leaves, has grown well above
the top of the holder, supported by
its special aerial roots. There are
two 6 litre (1½ gallon) HYDRO-
TANKS fitted at either end of this
unit and LEWATIT HD 5 is used for
easy, long-term care.

Picture acknowledgements
BASF-Landwirtschaftliche
Versuchsanstalt Limburgerhof /
Rheinpfalz:- 116, 117(2), 118,
119(2), 120(2), 121; Hans R. Brost,
Leverkusen:- 9; Brune
Luftbefeuchtung, Ludwigshafen /
RH.:- 99; GEPE Hydrotechnik,
Karlsruhe:- 21(2); Gossen GmbH,
Erlangen:- 100; Dr. Hans Jesse,
Köln:- 22; LUWASA Interhydro AG,
Bern:- 6, 53, 55, 77; Jolanthe
Nolde, Heidelberg:- 73; Otto-
Hydropflanzen, Mannheim:- 89;
TWL International, Hydrokultur
GmbH, Rüsselsheim:- 23, 54, 59,
78 (top).
All other pictures:- Dr. Wolfgang
Blaicher, Mannheim.

Graphics:- Hellmut Hoffman,
München.

Contents

Preface

This up-to-the-minute book is a concise, to-the-point source of reference and will provide invaluable advice and information on the use of hydroponics in the home. It is, unfortunately, imperative to keep a critical distance from much of what is said and written about hydroponics — even by supposed experts. In this respect "ABC of Hydroponics" will prove indispensable.

The majority of the photographs in this book are of plants I have owned for many years and, this being the case, they provide proof that hydroponics really is a means of ensuring the health and longevity of your plants. An attempt has been made to graphically show how the various procedures necessary to promote the wellbeing of your plants are carried out.

The HYDRO-TANK patented by Dr. Blaicher, who also supplied the photographs for this book, has been such a world-wide success and had such an impact on hydroponics that nobody could possibly disapprove of its frequent mention in this book. Suggestions made by the editorial staff of the German magazine *Mein Schöner Garten (My Beautiful Garden)* led to the successful transgression into the field of "useful" plants, discussed on pages 104/5 and 107. This too would have been impossible without the HYDRO-TANK. However, I would like to end this preface on an important note: the advice and criticism made in this book should not be taken the wrong way, but used to the full, to help you meet the demands of soilless culture, the science which is still so full of potential.

I would like to thank BLV Publishers Ltd, for their understanding help.

Margot Schubert (text)
Dr. Wolfgang Blaicher (photographs)

This rustic-style circular holder by LUWASA (series "Hydroponics"; model, ETERNIT 2000) carries a guarantee for its protective inner coating. (See page 22)

From soil to hydroponics

Practical introduction

Even a small book needs something along the lines of an introduction. After all, however practically orientated your interest in hydroponics is, it is still desirable to know some of its historic background; to know why, about 100 years ago, we even thought of abandoning the use of soil in certain areas of plant cultivation. The early history of hydroponics goes right back to Aristotle, who lived about 350 BC. But for almost 2,000 years very little progress was made in this field, and what development there was, was purely incidental. For European scholars were researching into very different matters other than how one might allow plants to grow and flourish without soil and with only a nutrient solution. . . . In about 1840 Justus von Liebig propounded the unequivocable mineral nature of plant nutrition in his *"Agrikulturchemie"*. He did not however take the final step in drawing the practical consequences of his discovery, which we today can see as closely related.

This task was reserved for the two professors Knopp and Sachs who, in about 1860, produced the so-called Knoppian solution. In this solution Professor Sachs in Bonn, Germany, grew for the first time that famous maize plant (see diagram below).

Professor Sach's famous maize plant, grown in the so-called Knoppian solution.

If it is incontestable that the first stages of the development of hydroponics took place in Germany, then it is America that has to be credited with the next major steps forward. These occurred during the middle of the First World War and remained virtually unknown in Germany for over a decade later. In his book *"Soilless Gardening"*, published in 1940, Professor W.F. Gericke refers to experiments taking place in the States since 1929, partly under the name "hydroponics". All these together formed the basis for the utilization of the "hydroponic systems" which

Amazing but true — a hydroponicist friend of mine has been growing tomato plants for years in a small polythene foil greenhouse. He always harvests an abundant crop of very aromatic fruit. The necessary nutrients are supplied by a 50 litre (14 gallon) HYDRO-TANK.

were developed for vegetable cultivation on Ascension Island, the highly important American military base in the middle of the Atlantic, 1,300 km (800 miles) north-west of St. Helena. Today this would all have little more than historical significance, were it not for the fact that Professor Gericke considered precisely those questions and problems with which we too shall be concerned.

In the '50s attempts in Germany to grow "useful plants" failed almost at the very beginning due to financial difficulties. Now, however, the application of hydroponics to "useful" plants and outdoor gardening is spreading in Europe too *(see page 102).*

And now, before we finish this introduction, just a little information on the name "hydroponics". All plant lovers

9

From soil to hydroponics

will know exactly what is meant by this term, but it may be somewhat confusing for the average man in the street — after all, there are many other terms beginning with the Greek word "hydro" = water; the term "ponics" also originates from the Greek — "ponos" = labor. Hydroponics then, for those who do not know, refers to the science of growing plants without using soil and supplying the necessary nutrients in the form of a solution impregnated with mineral salts and trace elements. Sometimes it is also called "soiless culture" or "nutriculture". In Germany the term "Hydrokultur" (hydro-culture) is used.

Why choose hydroponics?

To make the purpose of this book clear, we must first pose the above question. Hydroponics, as is true of everything, must be practised with a certain expertise to make it worthwhile. So this book has been written to help and show you how to do things properly, so you can fully profit from the advantages hydroponics affords both you and your plants. There are indeed great advantages to be gained and it is for this reason that more and more

people are turning to hydroponics, even if it means changing old habits they acquired while growing their plants in soil. Since the mid-70s, a great deal of research and development into various related fields has brought about substantial advances in hydroponics. Insight has been gained into many technical and botanical details. However, there is still plenty of scope for plant lovers to discover further faults and failings and overcome them or bypass them according to their personal experience.

Everybody will soon discover for himself that it is fairly easy to practise hydroponics at home and that he may even be able to enrich the subject further by his own ideas.

It must be said that the biggest dangers plants grown hydro-ponically have to face are insufficient or excess water supply.

The problem of unreliable water-level indicators has still to be solved, as indeed can be said for the unsatisfactory shape of many of the smaller hydroponic containers. So, the field is still wide open for anyone who is sufficiently interested and enterprising.

From soil to hydroponics

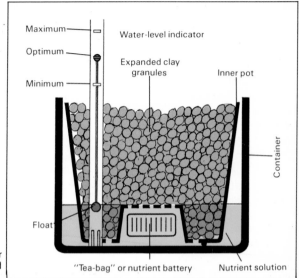

Maximum — Water-level indicator

Optimum —

Minimum —

Expanded clay granules

Inner pot

Container

Float

"Tea-bag" or nutrient battery

Nutrient solution

Vertical cross-section of a hydroponic container with its inner pot and water-level indicator.

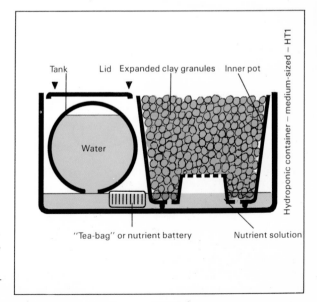

Tank   Lid   Expanded clay granules   Inner pot

Water

Hydroponic container – medium-sized – HT1

"Tea-bag" or nutrient battery

Nutrient solution

Vertical cross-section of the HYDRO-TANK. Left, the tank; right, the inner pot; note the absence of a water-level indicator.

From soil to hydroponics

The dangers of growing plants in the same pot.

It is because we are all confirmed hydroponicists that we can safely broach this less pleasant subject at the beginning of the book. Traditionally grown plants have always been available in magnificent arrangements in pots and baskets. The contents of these pots, however, usually soon die or can be only just saved by separating the individual plants and providing them with a pot of their own — a fate which is known to be inevitable from the very start. Amongst professional hydroponicists long-term "cohabitation" has become the

This combination of plants in the same unit was, on delivery, still elegant and attractive. Before the year was out, however, the fast growing *Ficus pumila* had "taken over" to such an extent that the delicate *Dizygotheca*, which has highly sensitive roots, had not developed any new shoots. The future of these two plants is obvious.

vogue, both for small units (from the 11cm (4in) pot upwards) and those intended for tables. This idea was probably conceived as an analogy to the practice of mixing the plants in larger units. The desired decorative effect is all important and no allowance is made for the requirements of the individual plants and their growth rate — the combination must be striking and impressive. Admittedly such an arrangement of plants may be more effective than the more silent beauty of a single plant, but the eagerness to conform to public demand at the expense of common sense has gradually been taken to an extreme. Cases can be found where two plants in a 15cm (6in) pot (see picture bottom left) fight each other for space, light and food until the weaker one dies. Given this, the widely practised arranging of three to four plants in a 15cm (6in) pot is simply totally and utterly irresponsible. All the more so, since anybody with experience must know that, when the plants grow, a jungle of roots will be the consequence.

This practice challenges the major advantage hydroponics has otherwise over growing plants in soil, as regards repotting.

These plants have been combined without any consideration for growth rate or root development. Back left, *Areca* palm; back right, Mistletoe Fig; front left, the succulent *Somona*; front right, *Crytanthus* which originates from tropical rain forests.

What's more, today you can even buy ground creepers as standard accompaniment plants, yet these are veritable 'killers'. Such examples are *Ficus Pumila,* climbing *Philodendrons* and the Variegated Wax Plant, of which there is now also a green cultivar. I have actually seen an *Areca* Palm and a Stag's horn fern paired off with ivy. It should not come as a surprise either that a *Codiaeum* (Croton), a *Scindapsus* or a succulent *Euphorbia* just simply cannot be grown together.

13

Growth Factors

If you ask in hydroponics specialist shops what kind of ground knowledge their clients have as regards house-plants, then the answer will always be the same — very few are totally ignorant. In fact, the opposite seems to be true: the more experienced they are in growing potted plants, the keener they are to "try out" hydroponics, after all, this way everything is supposed to look after itself!

But everything does not look after itself. Otherwise you would neither require thorough advice when buying your equipment and plants, nor this book to guide you.

But if you do have a basic general knowledge of house-plants, this will help you understand the prerequisites for all plants, whether grown hydroponically or in soil. The need for light, air, warmth, water and food remains the same, only the provision of the latter two is, in hydroponics, very different and decisive for the easy, long-term care of the plant. If carried out correctly, the expert will class these conditions as "optimal". *Hydroponics always provides plants of all growth rates with their optimal needs and in an easily absorbable form.*

Thus, providing your plant with the correct place to stand is more important than all else — hence our devoting a whole page to this subject (see opposite).

As usual, the information provided there cannot be taken as a hard and fast rule. There is a great deal of flexibility where the values North / South / East / West merge into each other. Nevertheless, with a bit of effort, you can avoid the worst mistakes if you follow this rough guide together with the advice given in the chapter on our selection of plants (see p.52 ff.) and other relevant information.

Of course, judging from experience, plants looked after "optimally" are not adversely affected by a temporary (at the most a few days) decrease in their required light intensity. It is always bad for your plant — but especially in the winter — if it is standing in direct contact with a cold stone floor. We have also recently learned that a heated floor with a temperature of about 30°C (86°F) can have damaging consequences. The normal temperature for house-plants which are not dormant should be 18-20°C (64-68°F). Dormant plants, whose water-level has been reduced almost to

Position and direction faced

North
(approx. north-north-west to
north-north-east)

Advantages. Provided no shadow thrown
by obstacles, all the advantages of
"light" shade and balanced temperature.
Best position for all plants that must have
shade, including those from tropical rain
forests. No additional shading necessary.
Disadvantages. Light intensity can be
impaired by obstacles outside
window – e.g. large trees and buildings.
The shadow may then be too deep for
many plants. If in a vulnerable position,
beware of temperature of nutrient
solution falling too low and protect plants
from "cold feet". Protect from outside
walls and windows. For heating see
chapter headed "Looking after your
plants".

East
(approx. north-north-east to
east-south-east)

Advantages. Mild, morning sun, good for
growth. Northerly and southerly
directions provide a wide scope for
grouping different plants. Good for all
plants which tend to prefer half-shade.
Best position for recently transferred
plants to re-adapt to new environment
and for seedlings and newly acquired
plants to acclimatize.
Disadvantages. Northerly
direction – may be affected by weather
conditions and cold. If strong sunshine,
will need shading. If trees, etc., outside
act as required screen, remember to
compensate for loss of leaves in winter, if
necessary.

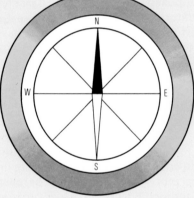

West
(approx. west-south-west to
north-north-west)

Advantages. Only positions which face
more toward north will receive rays of
late-afternoon and evening sun and thus
be suitable for plants requiring large
amount of light and heat.
Disadvantages. If in direct sunlight
facing west and west-south-west, then
beware same dangers as for plants facing
south – window panes heat up
excessively and cool off too fast at night.
For northerly directions, remember that
often same disadvantages as for north.
Bad position for young plants to gather
strength and healthy plants which are
delicate to sudden temperature changes.

South
(approx. east-south-east to
west-south-west)

Advantages. Apart from longest daylight
hours and greatest light intensity – none.
Disadvantages. Only safe for plants if
overcast sky, unless shading can be
provided when necessary. Full sun
dangerous even for cacti and other
succulents from desert areas because
window panes heat up too much. In
winter greater contrast between day and
night temperatures – beware of "cold
feet"!
N.B. Always provide awnings on outside.
Make sure you can regulate intensity of
light entering room. Constant, deep
shade from blind is more detrimental to
plant than the darkest northern shade.

Growth Factors

zero, will manage with less warmth.

The lower the water-level in the container, the cooler the allowed temperature of the nutrient solution.

This applies particularly to the resting period of cacti and other succulents, for rooted bulbs (e.g. Amaryllis), for the Passion Flower and for the Wax Plant, which you are supposed to put aside at a temperature of 5-6°C (41-42°F). But to return to the main growth factors.

Light — not to be confused with the use of artificial light, which is discussed elsewhere — is one of the most important factors for plant life.

Light provides the energy for the complex chemical process of photosynthesis, through which the plant converts carbon dioxide and water to food (in the form of sugars). Also necessary are the inorganic substances which in hydroponics are supplied directly by the nutrient solution. The colour of leaves and flowers also directly corresponds to the light conditions, especially when variegated leaves turn green. And we must not forget that house-plants in their natural environment are accustomed to very different light intensities than we can provide, even under the best circumstances. On the other hand, African Violets, leaf Begonias and other favorites from the tropical rain forests cannot take either direct sunlight or too much light. However ideal other factors in hydroponics may be, they cannot counterbalance bad light conditions. So, when you are buying a plant, however much you may like it, you should first carefully consider whether you can fulfil the conditions it requires and only then buy it. Hydroponically grown plants, just like those grown in soil, are subject to phototropism (i.e. growing towards the light) and thus liable to lose their flower buds if you turn or move them. Thus large hydroponic units on castors or rollers do not only have advantages but also tempt you to move the plant about, often without giving the matter much thought. To avoid unintentional rotation of smaller units, use a location marker. This should be attached to the edge of the inner pot and not to the outside of the holder. A practical tip — use a cocktail stick that is resistant to the nutrient solution to mark the direction of the light, that is, if the water-level indicator cannot

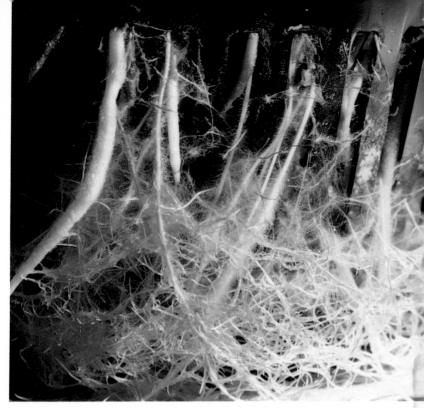

Roots of a Christmas Narcissus. As an experiment the plant was grown throughout the year (ignoring its usual resting period) in a 15cm (6in) pot; HYDRO-TANK HT1. The water-level was kept at 2cm (1in). In the picture you can clearly see the contrast between the roots in contact with the nutrient solution and those growing in the moist air.

be used to do this.

Finally, take a look at the picture of roots shown above − here there are still some interesting points to make as regards "watering" and water-level. These roots have grown in a constant, low water-level and reveal in their structure that the old habit of alternating the water-level between high and low is not one to which they are naturally adapted. Above the water-line you can see the very fine root hairs which are adapted to absorb air-moisture, while below are the smooth, thicker roots with their innumerable, also smooth, lateral roots which grow into the nutrient solution and prefer to stay there.

Note. For the growth factors which have not been dealt with in detail, please see p.40 ff. and p.88 ff.

Hydroponic containers

The inner pot

As regards pots, those used in hydroponics really are superior to all others. For despite its modest appearance, the so-called inner pot plays a decisive role in the whole execution of hydroponics. As well as keeping the same standard sizes and slightly tapering shape as the traditional flower pot, it too serves the function of providing space in which the roots can grow, albeit in this case under totally different conditions. The groove in the base is designed to hold a nutrition battery. It is of great importance that the material used is perfect for our particular needs. In other words, the inner pot and the inner lining of the hydroponic container must be resistant to the nutrient solution. If this requirement is not met, chemical reactions may take place which are dangerous to plants.

The second problem lies in the range of design as regards the openings in the wall of the inner pot. The model with the five narrow slits is most frequently available in the shops. Supposedly it prevents excessive root growth, but

Inner pots for small and medium sized containers — standard size 12cm (5in). Back row, for large containers — standard size 20cm (8in). Front right, latticed nursery pots and SCHLITZI — size usually 6cm (2½in).

Hydroponic containers

A colorful selection of modern hydroponic containers — standard sizes 12 and 20 cms (5 and 8ins). Diameter and volume depends on the model; suitable for 11, 15 and 18cm (4, 6 and 7in) pots.

damage is almost inevitable to the roots when the inner pot has to be removed from its holder. This design also restricts their ventilation. The THOVADEC-pot with its wide slits (bottom left) undoubtedly provides better conditions for growth. A latticed design like the white VETTER-pot (middle front) is dangerous to the roots when it is removed from a narrow holder. If, however, there is a great deal of surrounding space, as in the case of the HYDRO-TANK, these pots are ideal, both for root growth and aeration.

A review of hydroponic containers

This review must inevitably begin with a comment on the great variety of very different models. There are small and medium-sized holders (ideal for standing on tables) for inner pots with diameters of 9-18cms (3½in-7in) and their corresponding standard sizes.

Hydroponic containers

Along with a decorative purpose, one can detect in all these cases a desire for a utilitarian design of the shape — that is, one that does not confine the plant to a small cylindrical space and thereby restrict even further the already limited room for root formation. This dual function began to dominate design when the famous rectangular holder by LUWASA, in Wiesbaden, West Germany, appeared on the market and the first major trend in man-made materials was also catching the imagination of designers — for example the team GLASENAPP – WÜNNENBERG. Incidentally, many of these, albeit with slight alteration, are still available in the shops although changing public tastes has meant that much of the market has now been taken over by ceramic holders. The latter are in no way technically superior but are simply considered more "stylish". Nevertheless, ceramicware does really deserve more attention than plastic because there can be no fear of chemical reactions with the nutrient solution.

However, for both materials it is true to say that buying cheap, poor quality goods may have dire consequences.

In ceramic-ware, invisible hair-line cracks in the glazing allow the nutrient solution to penetrate the holder itself and produce dangerous chemical reactions by releasing soluble toxic compounds. Some manufacturers of high quality ceramics safeguard against this risk by using a double coat of glazing.
Polystyrene (PS) which is the most frequently used man-made

The "mini" HYDRO—TANK is the smallest hydroponic unit available. It is ideal for growing young plants, small succulents, cuttings and for germinating seeds. Here it holds a young cucumber plant which was grown from two pips. The plant also remained a miniature and flowered beautifully for three months. For further details see page 30ff.

Hydroponic containers

material for inner pots and all other containers, can be used without hesitation.

Products, such as the large containers by VIESSMAN made of polyurethane (PUR) are also ideal. You can distinguish them from just any old plastic household or garden object by their special, hand-finished surface. A great deal of damage has resulted from adapting common household and garden containers to hydroponics. This damage ranges from leaves falling off, roots rotting and general growth deficiency to the total death of the plant.

The same warning applies to the use of metal containers — be they brass, copper or pewter. All react with the nutrient solution and thus release dangerous toxins.

"Nutrient resistant varnish", supposedly a safety coating, does not provide real protection, because the inevitable wear may cause fatal hair-line cracks in the protective coating.

Above, large containers (RU 50). Left, planted with a *Yucca elephantipes;* right, selection of colors available. Below; left, yellow box-like container (RE 70); middle front, round, red container (RU 70); behind, brown, square model with *Dracaena fragans massangeana;* right, white, hexagonal holder (SE 70).

Hydroponic containers

This also applies to the large "rustic" models, which are becoming increasingly popular for larger plants. This popularity is no surprise, seeing that the series "Hydroponics" ETERNIT 2000 already leaves the factory with an inner protective varnish, which carries the manufacturer's guarantee. (See picture page 6).

As for the viability of calcium-based materials such as marble, one should be aware that the stylish exterior (see picture page 59) conceals a chemical resistant lining which is reinforced with glass fibre. These elegant pots are made of three segments so that they cannot be criticized even on account of their weight. Incidentally, glass containers are also sometimes available on the market, but these are merely a fashion fad. They are hardly suitable for hydroponics because light can reach the roots which have grown through the inner pot. They also promote the growth of algae, which are very difficult to eradicate. The only possible remedy, and even then not without some reservation, is ALGIZIN, used for aquariums.

Right, handmade large ceramic containers are TWL International's new line. Here we have their nut-brown model MILOS; diameter 54cm (18in), height 21cm (8in). The wall is only slightly curved so it does not impair root growth. The tall *Yucca* tree and the variegated *Ficus benjamina* make a decorative combination. Whether the pairing together of the robust *Yucca aloifolia* and the more delicate *Ficus* will be successful in the long run must remain to be seen.
Left, large flower box, made to measure. The arrangement of plants, *Ficus benjamina*, Fern, *Anthurium*, Azalea in a clay pot with inner fitting; behind, Dracaena; right, Philodendron.

Accessories to help you

The water-level indicator

The water-level indicator is absolutely indispensable for all hydroponic containers of the usual kind. Those for small and middle-sized holders are highly unreliable, especially if they are already attached to the inner pot. Whoever uses these models must unfortunately always expect flaws in measurement and thus constantly carry out spot checks.

This is also true of the double-sectioned models by COMBI COR whose measuring instruments run sidewards along the top half of the holder on little rails. One such example can be seen in the middle row of the collection of containers on page 19 — next to the wicker-work holder. Another is used for the *Anthurium* on page 67, not however without careful monitoring and timely checking of the float. To facilitate the latter, there is a special moveable fitting. Today the unreliability of all these indicators is notorious — indeed, it almost appears that the structural deficiencies are inherent in the design and thus unalterable.

The water-level indicator consists of two tubes, the inner one containing the float. In order for the float to be able to move up and down according to the water-level in the holder, there must be openings through which the nutrient solution can enter the tube. LENI has brought out a protective cap with narrow slits, but even this cannot prevent bits of roots, LEWATIT and expanded clay granules from entering the tube along with the solution and thus preventing the mobility of the float.

On the other hand, the float needs a pocket of air at the top, which varies according to the rise and fall of the water-level, yet this promotes condensation. Up until now, the condensation could enter the inner tube without hindrance and at the same time run down its sides, which really did hinder the float's mobility.

For this reason some water-level indicators have recently been constructed with a float-rod which cannot alter its weight. But these too are subject to a second no less serious danger — the adhesion or potential

This picture shows a whole collection of water-level indicators, mainly for small and medium-sized containers. The water-level indicators designed for large containers — for example the large white model at the back — are considerably more reliable than their smaller counterparts and have a longer life-span.

Accessories to help you

adhesiveness of the tube or the rod to the damp wall of the top of the indicator. This happens especially frequently when the instrument is not totally upright. There are thus two dangers which may occur and both are equally damaging in their results.

1. The float remains stuck at the bottom, giving the warning that the plant is too dry and you should supply water immediately.

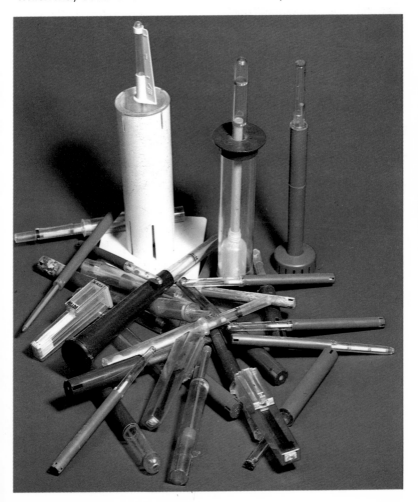

Accessories to help you

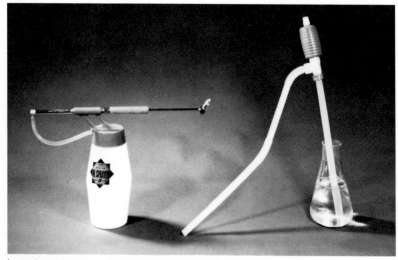

Large humidifiers are discussed on page 99. Here we are dealing with a practical hand model from Japan, which has a very unusual shape. Soon this spray will be indispensable for every plant lover. It can hold up to 1½ litres (2 quarts) of water and its spray nozzle can be easily directed as required. You can thus also aim directly at leaves from underneath, which is so urgently recommended as prevention against red spider mite — especially in the case of

And if you do not pay enough attention and constantly add more water until the container is flooded to the top, then the result will be very heavy, even fatal, root-damage.

2. As a result of sticking to the top of the float constantly indicates MAX. You therefore think the plant is well supplied, until the effects of drying out become visible.

Chamaedorea elegans. Of course nobody will purposely fill their hydroponic container right up to the brim with water, just because the indicator points to Minimum. But suppose it does happen. Then it would be ideal to have such a cheap, small pump at hand, which will remove excess water in a flash. If it becomes blocked the remedy is also very simple — just rinse it out. A battery operated pump is far more problematic.

Both incidences would occur less frequently if hydroponicists realized that, like everything, a water-level indicator is also subject to wear and tear and that it is better to water less than too much. For this reason more recent models no longer restrict themselves to indicating MAX. and MIN., but also show the mean — OPT. or BEST. But even this may be too high and the required level depends on

Accessories to help you

Rotted bamboo canes or wooden supports are discussed on page 91, where they are described as one of the potentially most dangerous cultural mistakes in hydroponics. At last, however, people are turning to better alternatives and above we have a few such examples. The collection ranges from a climbing frame and delicate supporting rods to much bigger supports which slot into each other. All are easily obtainable at hydroponics shops, so there is no excuse not to buy them. See page 91 for a picture of rotted supports.

the kind of plant, its position and growth rate. It is also very difficult to maintain low levels that alternate with MIN. and here the whole purpose of hydroponics may be lost.
The only other accessory that I shall mention now is a small watering can.

This *Iresine herbstii* (cf. page 109), having grown into a young plant, needed to be supported. Instead of using dangerous wooden rods I had the inspiration of using plastic drinking straws. They are ideal for this light-weight little plant, and, what's more, can be bought absolutely anywhere!

Accessories to help you

A flexible macramé net transforms even the 1 litre (quart) HYDRO-TANK, originally designed to stand on a table, into a practical hanging unit with a large water reservoir. For plant, see page 56.

Wall mounts and hanging baskets

These are depicted in such detail in the accompanying illustrations that very little remains to be said. Experience has shown that hanging hydroponic pots are always a bit more inconvenient than their standing counterparts – for obvious reasons. The problem is, however, lessened because hydroponics enables long-term plant-care. Removal of the pots from the flexible hangings has also become easier.

Three modern wall mounts and hanging baskets; left, a strong macramé net which ▶ can even hold heavy containers such as the beautiful 18cm (7in) ceramic model by LUWASA; right, a round water-resistant mat made of SKAI by TWL which can be pulled apart by its cord to form the holder, here depicted with a red hydroponic container; middle, a delicate design made of nylon and shells intended for light-weight containers.

Accessories to help you

The thermometer

This important accessory must not be forgotten. You insert it into the specially designed opening found in most inner pots or in the holder. The temperature of the nutrient solution can easily be read off on the scale. You *must* possess a thermometer — you need it for the general care of your plants, as well as for forcing and for propagation.

A new way – the HYDRO-TANK

The stimulus for the development of Dr. Blaicher's HYDRO-TANK was provided by the weaknesses and failings of previous hydroponic systems. That is –

1. The entire watering system of the older designs does not correspond to the insights we have gained today of the relationships between root-growth, nutrient solution levels and oxygen requirements in the hydroponic pot and its growing medium. The small cylindrical containers, unfortunately so popular with many buyers and so detrimental to the healthy growth of the plant, also contribute to the problem – never mind the frequent overcrowding of the pot, which was discussed earlier. And to top it all, should the hydroponicist, out of the goodness of his heart, decide to give his plants a "little extra" solution rather than too little, then the seeds of destruction are already sown.

2. The unreliability of the water-level indicator has hitherto remained unresolved. Perhaps you ought to turn back to the chapter on accessories and reread from page 24 onwards, to remind yourself of dangers. It must be said, that even the better constructed models for the large hydroponic containers, which are primarily superior because of their permanent fixture, can fail, especially if the system has been going for some time. If this failure is not noticed soon enough it will lead to problems which may even result in the death of your plants.

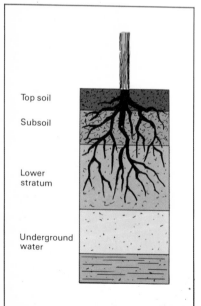

Top soil

Subsoil

Lower stratum

Underground water

A vertical cross-section of soil strata from a gardening book. This shows that, in their natural state too, tree roots do not actually grow in water, but draw up a constant supply of moisture through their growing medium.

A new way – the HYDRO-TANK

The medium-sized HYDRO-TANK which is ideal as a table decoration. Left, container with the axle bearings to hook in the rotatable tank (middle); right, the lid to cover the tank which can be tipped downwards when necessary. The unit is suitable for any 15cm (6in) pot. Size, L. 280mm (11in), W. 165mm (6½in), H. 133mm (5½in).
Diagram (a) roots without water, no decrease in air retention capacity of growing medium; (b) low water-level; no serious loss of air spaces; (c) too high a water-level, dangerous reduction in the roots' air supply.

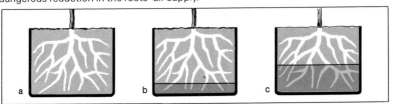

A new way – the HYDRO-TANK

If the new HYDRO-TANK were only to free us from the dangers of an unreliable water-level indicator it would already be worth our attention. However, it has many other advantages. Perhaps not every one will enthuse about the shape of the 1 litre (1 quart) table unit, but if it is a question of aesthetics or good results and long-term convenience, then the former can hardly bear any relevance. After all, the 1 litre (1 quart) tank must be accommodated somehow otherwise, without a reservoir, you would not be able to maintain the requisite low water-level without constant surveillance. And one does have a choice of colors – the containers come in brown or beige. Now, to discuss the HYDRO-TANK's other advantages.

The new unit guarantees each plant – including the inevitable second plant – in a 15cm (6in) inner pot a certain degree of freedom upwards through the compulsory spacing.

Above, the 1 litre (quart) installable HYDRO-TANK. It is made up of a rectangular container with the axle bearings, a rotatable tank and lid for the 'camouflage' of expanded clay granules.

Below, the above unit containing two *Somona* ''Gabriela'' hybrids, which flower unceasingly. Both are supplied by the same tank yet grow separately.

A new way – the HYDRO-TANK

The same applies to the three installable tank units shown in this chapter. The space taken up by the tanks themselves is often camouflaged within a few months of growth. One example – can you see any trace of the container for the rotatable tank in the photograph on page 61?

However, the HYDRO-TANK too has been developed further.

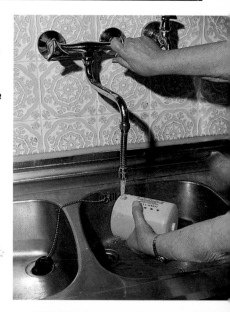

The "Mini Tank" is the smallest of these tank units, measuring only 115 × 65 × 60mm. (4 ½ × ½ x 2in). It was already mentioned on page 20. There is again a choice of colors – dark brown or beige.
Since many of the plants gradually outgrew their Mini Tank, yet they were still too small to be transferred to the 1 litre (1 quart) unit, an intermediate size was developed – the ½ litre (1 pint) tank unit. The most recent innovation is the nursery tray, which is ideal for kitchen herbs, seedlings of any kind and as a cacti garden.

Above, the tank can be filled or topped up at any time with water from the cold tap. It releases so little of this water into the container at one go, that the temperature evens itself out without damage to the plant.

Below; left, another "mini" tank unit with a small *Aloe mitriformis;* right, the new half litre (1 pint) unit

A new way – the HYDRO-TANK

The S-tank, fitted into a table unit, is in this case set at 5mm (¼ in) (!) for the growing, flowering *Phalaenopsis*.

The water-level maintainable by the S-tank ranges from 0-30mm (1¼ in) and can be precisely adjusted. To do so, just follow the scale printed on the tank.

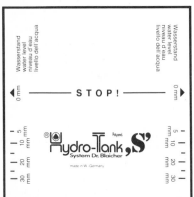

Apart from the normal tank, there is now also the S-tank for table units, which can maintain an even lower water-level. But more on this subject in the chapter "Using the new hydropinic unit", page 102ff.

In the table unit with a 1 litre (1 quart) tank the normal water-level is 20mm (¾ in) (in exceptional cases, when going away etc., this can be raised up to 50mm (2in)). The S-tank enables you to maintain a water-level of only 0-30mm (1¼ in).

The plant is in no way impeded from drawing as much water as it needs during periods of growth and dormancy from the store in the tank. The frequency of refilling the tank after opening the aperture for the water supply increases accordingly. However the all important humidity between the expanded clay granules will always remain constant, for the superior quality of these granules provides the required degree of capillary attraction. This, together with the other factors mentioned, gives Dr. Blaicher's hydroponic systems their superiority over all others. In the case of large hydroponic units, the usual intervals for supplying the water increases by several weeks depending on the plant(s).

A new way – the HYDRO-TANK

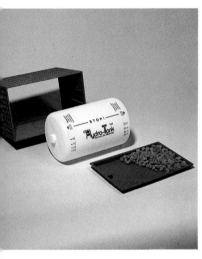

The 6 litre (1½ gallon) installable tank can be built into any large unit with a diameter or length of more than 65cm (26in). It can be fitted either before or after planting. The measurements of its frame are L. 305mm (12in), W. 190mm (7½in), H. 210mm (8in). The 2 litre (½ gallon) installable tank, same model as above, is designed for "small large" units, which have a length or diameter of more than 35cm. (14in). Its measurements are L. 190mm (7½in), W. 110mm (4in), H, 210mm (8in).

No watering from above is required and the tank can be topped up at any time – it does not have to be empty. Removal is extremely easy, especially for the table units.
On the subject of use and further developments, see "Using the new hydroponic unit", page 102ff.

The growing medium

If you ask hydroponicists the name of those somewhat irregularly shaped, brownish balls which they use instead of soil, you will always be given a different answer; namely diverse brand-names. But what is meant is always one and the same — expanded clay granules. This is a structurally stable, non-decomposable lightweight material used as a growing medium in hydroponics. It has now dominated this market since the mid-sixties. In the building trade Leca has been its official abbreviation for a long time and today, even in the sphere of hydroponics, is still a sign of high quality. Leca means Light Expanded Clay Aggregate and is also a brand-name.

Clay, an ancient composite already known in biblical times and earlier, varies in its chemical make-up and physical properties according to its origin. Only the clay used here has the property of expanding at a particular temperature and countless air bubbles form in the otherwise heavy clay. It is this structure that provides the capillary attraction required in hydroponics.

The manufacture of these porous balls from the disintegration of the dense raw

The growing medium

clay through the "rising" process is far from simple. After various preparatory treatments, the natural product is put into a special 80m (240ft) long, partitioned oven, and in this the clay balls "rise" during the baking process, at a temperature of 1,200°C (2,192°F). Though it is sometimes believed that expanded clay granules are made with the aid of pressurized air, it is in fact the reaction of the heat with the clay's carbonates, which produces this unique structure so conducive to the passage of water and air in the roots of hydroponic plants. This also means that the granules do not easily become water-logged. But why is it that a product used as a supplementary material for light-weight concrete construction and isolation in the building trade has found application in hydroponics? Seeing that this innovation practically revolutionized hydroponics — as did the

This individual granule of expanded clay clearly shows how the clay has expanded from within and how the surface is imperfectly formed.

The vertical cross-section reveals the irregular pores and their high capacity for retaining air.

The growing medium

Put in water, the expanded clay granules predominantly float on the surface and this test indicates that this aggregate is still the best growing medium available for hydroponics in the home.

speaking are the master stroke in the advancement of modern hydroponics. Until, that is, the young Swiss Gerhard Baumann came along. He worked in his father's building business near Bern, but in his spare time he was what we would call a plant fanatic. He wanted nothing more than to perfect the inadequate pre-war American hydroponic systems. And so, by way of an experiment, he came upon Leca, thus finding an alternative growth medium which was to become a great success.

He experimented with it for a long time, since apart from Leca's advantageous lightness — only 700kg per m^3 compared to the 1500kg of the same volume of basalt chippings, it did need to have other positive qualities to be of lasting use in hydroponics. At first it was purely a question of distinguishing between the cheaper Leca used as a supplementary material in the building trade and the chemically perfect, high quality Leca intended for horticultural application.

Today we must still be aware of the distinction.

Our recent insight into the decisive role played by the expanded clay granules in providing a constant supply of

introduction of the deionizer LEWATIT HD5 some ten years later — we must not be allowed to forget the series of events which led up to this decisive step.

Very few people will still remember what terrible problems the pioneers of hydroponics had to face before the discovery of expanded clay granules, through being restricted to the use of basalt chippings and quartz gravel. Already because of their weight, one hardly dared dream of large hydroponic units, which, strictly

The growing medium

oxygen to plant roots has proved to be of the greatest significance. This role is possible due to the dualism of Leca's physical properties. On the one hand the silicon dioxide (SiO_2), which is a major component, rejects water, while the pores naturally absorb water and also allow it to evaporate easily. This potential to retain both air and water with ease is vital to the well-being of roots.

Of course, the expanded clay granules can only fulfil their function if they are neither left completely dry (see top diagram) nor filled up with too much water (see bottom diagram). And again we reach the conclusion that the former practice of alternately leaving the plant to dry out too much and then soaking it in one go, or simply "drowning" it through constantly filling the container to the brim, does not do our plants any good. The ideal state is a constant low water-level, as shown in the middle diagram.

Above, the water has dried up completely and there is no humidity in the air spaces between the granules. For many plants this can be fatal.
Middle, constant low water-level of about 20mm (¾in); throughout the growing medium, optimal humidity level.
Below, water-level at 50mm (2in)+. Aggregates immersed in water are unable to hold air and roots suffer.

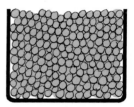

No nutrient solution

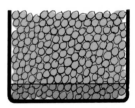

Depth of nutrient solution, 20mm (¾in)

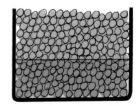

Depth of nutrient solution, 50mm (2in)

From water to nutrient solution

Unfortunately, before discussing how water is made into nutrient solution, we must begin by stating the obvious — water can vary greatly from area to area and, depending on its hardness or softness, may not always be suitable for our purposes. Experience has long taught us that hard water may demand special attention, otherwise it will ruin household appliances etc. Similarly you will find again and again that particular plants will, depending on the soil mixture, only grow well if they are given soft or softened water. As for example in the case of Azalias, Camelias and Philodendrons and other plants originating from the tropical rain forests. Once it was no problem to meet these requirements, — you could always use rain water.

Today, because of dangerous pollution levels, rainwater and snow must NOT be used, either for hydroponics or for watering any other plants.

The only exception is if you filter the water/snow through activated charcoal but who would honestly go to this trouble. . . . Anyway, we do not want to complicate the matter unnecessarily and without going into the even more complicated subject of pH values, suffice it to say that if the water from the mains (pipes) is less than 8° dH then you may follow the traditional method of making the nutrient solution. This method has, since the consolidation of hydroponics, become a clearly defined system.

Soft water from about 8° dH down can be safely used to make up the nutrient solution with the aid of mixtures that are commercially available for this purpose.

Of course the other option is to chemically soften the hard water and thus fulfil the requirements for the traditional method. Ready-made mixtures are only suitable to use if they contain no added fertilizers. This used to be true for the highly esteemed AQUISAL. Unfortunately, along with changing its name to FLEUR WATERSOFT, it has added the same fertilizers which we can find in AQUASOFT by COMPO and other such products. All are thus of no use in hydroponics. By the way, as a hydroponicist you should, strictly speaking, avoid using the words to "water" and "fertilize" in reference to hydroponics, to prevent confusion with the methods employed in growing

From water to nutrient solution

MERCKOQUANT strips for testing the hardness of water. The strips have 'zones' which, when dipped in water, indicate its hardness by changing color. No change in all four, softest water possible, under 3° dH; change in one, soft water between 4-7° dH; two, average hardness, 8-14° dH; three hard water 16-21° dH; all four, very hard water, above 23° dH. After opening, close the tube immediately; pay attention to the use by date. Also see pages 42 and 44.

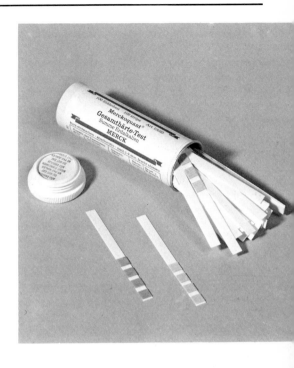

plants in soil. Admittedly this is not always possible but you should at least always bear the distinction in mind. In hydroponics, the plants receive nutrients which are especially put together for their specific situation. These are richer than the usual plant fertilizers.

Although nutrients used in hydroponics are also good for plants grown in earth, common fertilizer cannot be used in hydroponics.

All these points must be made in some detail, because there are still many hydroponicists who live in areas with soft water and who thus still favour the traditional method. Or perhaps they can obtain distilled water without great expense. After all, as was once the case with rain water, this frees them from any worries about the hardness of the water and other such problems — especially undesirable salt residues. The liquid concentrates and their powder counterparts, which are

From water to nutrient solution

now less popular, contain diverse minerals such as calcium, potassium, magnesium sulphate, phosphate and iron along with other growth stimulants in the form of trace elements and vitamins. The plant absorbs these nutrients and in doing so, salt residues always remain behind in the solution. With time this may have an adverse effect on the plant.

Hence the rule — clean the container carefully every time you provide a fresh supply of nutrient solution.

Here we are really encroaching upon the subject of general care. This may be cheaper if you are following the traditional method, but it does involve considerably more work than if you were using a deionizer.

The MERCKOQUANT strips shown and discussed on pages 41 and 42, and especially those used for testing the nitrate level of the nutrient solution, are becoming more and more important in the practice of hydroponics at home. They are not, however, always stocked by specialist shops

The deionizer

Before concluding this chapter on water and nutrient solution with a review of the unique advantages of using a deionizer, there is one more obvious problem to be faced. Unfortunately it is one to which we cannot find a wholly satisfactory solution.
In one of the more recent books on hydroponics it says that you must be careful in using water from softening installations and that it is better to totally avoid using it in hydroponics. This warning applies to household water softening installations, which operate in different ways and may be detrimental to plants. At present I can only come up with two solutions to this problem. At home, where we have hard water, I have installed a tap which draws directly on the main supply, before it passes through the softening installation. And so I fetch the water for my plants bucket by bucket from this tap, which is in the cellar. Other hydroponicists will have to treck with their cans to friends who have no water softening installations — an ironic twist of modern technology.

From water to nutrient solution

On the other hand, hydroponicists who are able to use LEWATIT HD5 will encounter no difficulties.

To be suitable for using LEWATIT HD5, the water must have a hardness level of about 8-10°dH plus – this includes extremely high levels, although these are relatively rare.

Here it is better to feed the plant more sparingly, especially during the resting period.

But what actually is LEWATIT HD5? Because there are many different deionizers produced in the chemical industry (some also bear the generic name LEWATIT), one must always avoid confusion by using the more specific code HD5 to identify this particular product. LEWATIT HD5 consists of golden brown man-made granules which have been "loaded" with nutrients suitable for long-term plant care. In hard water LEWATIT HD5 transforms the dangerous excess of minerals into nutirents for the plant – in solvent form, of course.

Well known nutrient concentrates for use in the traditional method.
(a) Liquid (from left to right, HYDRAL, COMPO, TWL, LUWASA Vollnahrung).
(b) Powder, middle (HYDRAL and AGRIFLOR SUPER).

From water to nutrient solution

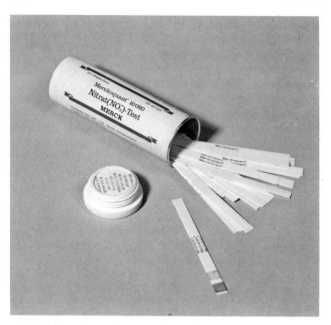

MERCKOQUANT nitrate test strips have made things a lot easier. There are two test zones; only the bottom one should change color when immersed in the nutrient solution, thus indicating the nutrient concentration. The color change ranges to deep purple. If the upper zone also changes, then this indicates the presence of nitrates as a result of contamination, having added too much water and other cultural errors. To remedy the situation, it is often sufficient just to lower the water level. All results can be analyzed with the aid of the color scale on the side of the tube. Again, remember to close the tube immediately after use and pay attention to the 'use by' date.

LUWASA also offers a preparation called LUWASA VOLLNAHRUNG for large and small hydroponic units. This is similar to LEWATIT HD5 but is supposed to work well even in the softest water. Then, however, you must remember that there will be a higher demand for nutrients.

As regards the required quantities and long-term effects of LEWATIT HD5, the general instructions provided can only be approximations. On average large plants need more than small ones; some, for example cacti and other succulents and

From water to nutrient solution

orchids too, naturally require less nutrients, especially during their resting period. It is best if you find out these requirements for yourself. It is quite easy to do so, with the aid of a MERCKOQUANT nitrate testing strip. At the same time you will be able to understand just why LEWATIT HD5 has meant such a step forward for hydroponics.

A lot of nonsense has already been circulated about LEWATIT HD5 and how it works. So let it be said, the granules neither consist of "hollow balls filled with fertilizer" which, when all the nutrients are absorbed would mean that empty shells were left behind, nor does the golden color of the granules turn black when the plant has absorbed all it requires.

When using LEWATIT HD5 you do not need to clean out your unit between each "feed". Some people have perfectly operational hydroponic units in which the LEWATIT HD5 has not been rinsed out for years, although this could be going a bit too far.

LEWATIT HD5 — the ideal nutrient for hydroponics developed by Bayer in about 1975, available in tins, packets and "tea-bags". Other firms now produce similar nutrients. Left, the three yellow 'caps' by LUWASA; right, BLUSANA by LENI; middle, two nutrient batteries to be fitted or jammed in the groove at the base of the inner pot.

Transferring to hydroponics

Taking risks as a hobby?

Today, when "ready-made" hydroponic units are easily available in plant shops, on markets and even through plant mail-order firms, transferring plants yourself from soil to hydroponic units is again coming into fashion. And yet, when the pioneers of hydroponics were still eagerly

awaiting the day when there would be hydroponic garden-centres, offering professionally set-up hydroponic units, I too once warned against the dangers of 'do-it-yourself transference'. Even in one of the latest books on hydroponics there is a chapter headed "Taking risks as a hobby?" But, in the meantime, one risk seems to have cancelled out the other — after all, in buying "ready-made" hydroponic units you are already taking certain chances.

If, however, you do the transferring yourself, and you do it properly, success is almost guaranteed. You will thus not risk the disappointment caused by someone else's mistakes.

You know exactly what has gone into your unit and the history of your plant. The fact that your plant will flourish is all the confirmation you require that all the risks you would have run, had you bought the unit from a shop, have been avoided.

This is how healthy a *Senecio macroglossus variegatus*, Cape Ivy, looked 3 months after being transferred to hydroponics. Its former pot had been too small (see pictures opposite). This plant is a succulent composite and has yellow flowers — naturally it is not in bloom here, having been transferred such a short time ago.

Transferring to hydroponics

Possible mistakes

Then again, the amateur might make serious mistakes in this operation which would easily have been avoided had he thought more "scientifically" about the work at hand. If a plant, previously grown in soil, is to overcome the undeniable risk of re-adaption, then it has to fulfil certain specifications.

Age, condition and growth rhythm of the plant play an important role in determining the success of the transference.

A plant should only be transferred at the time of the year when it is growing most rapidly. Preferably it should also not be more than

2-3 years old. Only then is it capable of abandoning its former root system and feeding habits and of switching from an organic to an inorganic life cycle. The transition period may often be problematic, but once this is overcome, the plant will flourish and draw full benefit from the indisputable advantages hydroponics affords. That is, providing these advantages are not negated by irresponsible watering.

The transference to hydroponics must be made when the plant is growing rapidly. For most plants this period of maximum growth is during the end of spring/early summer. Light, humidity and warmth are decisive factors.

The soil ball can be removed easily from the pot, which here is far too small for the plant, be carefully running a knife round the inside wall and soaking the whole pot and contents overnight.

Carefully remove the large lumps of soil and then place the roots in a bowl of lukewarm water, gradually removing more and more of the soil.

Transferring to hydroponics

When clean, rinse the roots off for the last time with lukewarm water, until no soil particles remain attached.

The plant had naturally divided into three sections; each of these is now clean and ready for transference.

Transference

The removal of the plant from its old flower pot often requires great care. On no account should the roots which protrude through the pot's drainage hole simply be cut away. Should the ball of soil adhere to the wall of the pot simply run a kitchen knife round the inside.

It is easiest to remove the ball of soil by giving the bottom of the pot a strong hit with a hammer. In this way there will be no damage done to the roots.

For then the base almost invariably breaks into two so that the plant can be removed without damaging the roots. Next you remove as much of the earth as possible by hand. At the same time begin to separate the larger roots from each other. Usually so much soil remains attached, especially to the more delicate root ends, that the roots have to be carefully rinsed and then placed in a container of slightly warmed water.

Even then, after soaking overnight, the fine roots which are vital for a successful transition to hydroponics may not be totally free of soil. In this case you have to continue rinsing them off gently – some people use their mouthwash for this purpose. The whole process may well take several days to complete properly. It would be ideal if the water used had a constant temperature of about 20-22°C (68-72°F), but this is scarcely possible without an

Transferring to hydroponics

The bottom of the inner pot is already filled with a layer of clay granules. First, the roots need to be trimmed.

Here the three sections of the plant are provisionally placed in the pot to see whether they are positioned correctly.

adjustable thermostat. From personal experience it suffices to avoid the damaging chills that result from using water straight from the cold tap. It is best to leave the water to stand until it reaches room temperature. Finally the roots will be free of all soil particles. But before "planting" into the prepared hydroponic pot and filling it up with clean expanded clay granules – NB use warm water to rinse them – you will have to go through the whole plant again with a pair of small pruning shears. Damaged or brown sections of the roots must be removed – the same applies to the foliage. Perhaps a few shoots will have to be trimmed to counterbalance the cutting of the roots.

This procedure is no different from that followed by all gardeners. When transplanting, the trimming of the roots always has to be paralled by a cutting back of the foliage.

The size of the inner pot has to be calculated generously, taking into account that you will need a smaller one for cacti and other slow-growing succulents, and a larger one for plants with a fast growth rate. Leave enough space that you will not have to transplant again in the too-near future. Then you need a layer of expanded clay granules at the bottom of the inner pot. The depth depends on the roots. Spread the roots out uniformly on this layer and be careful not to bend or break any.

Transferring to hydroponics

Above, fill the pot with clay granules up to the level to which the plant had previously been covered with soil. Continuously rotate and shake the pot. Below, transference completed.

Fill up the pot with the expanded clay granules, as shown in the picture at the top of page 50. It is best to use a measuring jug with a large lip.

Through continuously turning and lightly shaking the pot as you fill in the expanded clay granules, the roots and aggregate will naturally fall into place, leaving no large hollows. The plant will also have centred itself. It is totally wrong to press down the expanded clay granules as you would if they were potting soil. Here heavy root damage would result. Now the transference is completed and all that remains is the transition period and the successful growth of the first new shoot.

It is essential to place the plant in a warm, light — but not sunny — position and to watch the water-level with care. The roots have to adapt to their new environment and need moisture but not immersion in water, which would cause them to rot.

This *Stephanotis floribunda* has also been transferred from soil and again its previous pot had been far too small!

Our selection of plants

Some uninformed people may tell you that in all there are not more than a dozen house-plants which adapt well to hydroponics. Others reckon – and prove it through their professional concentration on this one field – that hydroponics should be restricted exclusively to evergreens because, as yet, there are no flowering plants which are really suitable. On the other hand optimists, judging by the large assortment of potted plants available, cheerfully claim that if you are skilled enough any plant can be grown hydroponically.

The truth, as always, is a compromise. Many plants can be grown hydroponically, but not always with an equal degree of success.

After all, the success of the plant depends on so many factors. The hydroponicist, however devoted and skilled, may make cultural errors, perhaps the position of the plant is not as good as it might be and finally, the plant itself may fail to do well on account of its individual prehistory – whether bought or not – and its own inability to adapt to a new environment. To avoid the latter risk you must select your plants with care. As regards the type of plant to be chosen – if you assume that every kind of plant could be grown hydroponically, you will surely be successful in the long run. And today your range of choice is larger than ever before. Since travel around the world has become so easy, new species and strains are constantly being introduced, especially in the field of hydroponics. These either turn out to be suitable or, after a short period of popularity, are again rejected. There can, however, be no real rules laid down as regards which plants should or should not be chosen.

For this reason, our selection of plants is merely a list of suggestions and makes no claims to being exhaustive.

What follows is based on my personal experience. Not everything will succeed the first time round and you will lose some plants, but some will flourish and last quite a few years, as is the case of the selection of large plants shown opposite.

Right, a decorative arrangement of two large units. The red top half of the back container provides a striking yet simple contrast to the modest collection of foliage plants. Dieffenbachia (front) and, towering behind, the very popular *Schefflera arboricola*. Collection by LUWASA.

Our selection of plants

Robust foliage plants

For an example of some robust foliage plants, you need only look at the picture opposite. The selection shown there has been carefully chosen to produce a varied effect. If you prevent the *Dieffenbachiae* from developing inflorescences by breaking them off every spring as soon as they form, then the manifoldly patterned leaves can grow unimpeded.

The small-leaved *Scheffera* **"Hong Kong"** also deserves a mention — it will not be infected by pests even if it is in a warm centrally heated room.

This *Spathiphllum wallisii* has grown so well that it is now in a "small" large container by TWL. If flowers magnificently, especially in hydroponics. It has a tendency to spread.

The plants in this selection of containers by LUWASA have each been given a pot of their own, in which they can grow unrestricted by any accessories. Left, *Chamaedorea elegans* (Parlour Plant); middle, Yucca Tree; right, a Croton (Codiaeum).

Among the larger **Araceae** (the Arum family), to which the **Dieffenbachiae** also belong, **Monstera**, the **Swiss Cheese Plant**, and **Philodendron** are perhaps the most important members. They will live many years, are very decorative, easy to propogate and present no problems as regards general care. Some species will even produce flowers quite readily. I would, however, strongly advise you against leave polishes, such as are often used for large-leafed plants. They are not only bad for the plants but make them look artificial.

All these plants will thrive if you do not move them from their position which, preferably, should be light but not sunny. Also do not chop at any aerial roots, and always keep to a regular routine.

The above picture is dominated

Our selection of plants

by a magnificent specimen of ***Yucca elephantipes***, **Spineless Yucca**, Like the ***Dracaena***, **False Palm** types, this is now most commonly grown as a cane cutting, with a crown of leaves at the side of the cane towards the top. These are also called **Ti Trees**. These often grow to be taller than a man, and are one of the most popular evergreens that are easy to look after and need a light/sunny position. The family of **Palms**, from ***Chamaedorea elegans,*** **Parlour Palm,** to the original **Coconut Tree** which grows from its nut, are also excellent for hydroponics.

A **Croton** requires a very low water-level but at the same time must have a great deal of humidity so that it does not lose its beautifully colored leaves. The specimen on page 33 even has an inflorescence.

Below and at the bottom of the next page you can see two recent ***Philodendron*** cultivars. There is, however, some confusion about their name. Botanists prefer to classify them as ***Monstera*** because their flowers cannot be significantly distinguished from the flowers of other plants belonging to this family. In the relevant captions we have used the botanical classification for these two cultivars but in the text itself they are referred to by their common name, which is also the one under which they are sold. The two pictures clearly demonstrate the wide range of different features that

Left, *Monstera friedrichsthalii*, a very attractive plant with delicate perforated leaves. These plants do, however, easily develop bare shoots. The only solution for this is to remove by pruning.

Right, a splendid new variegated cultivar called *Monstera deliciosa variegata* (it is sometimes mistakenly sold as Philodendron pertusum variegatum). It has a bushy growth, later gaining in height and requires a little more warmth than non-variegated varieties.

Our selection of plants

characterize the plants belonging to both these families. Indeed, these examples almost present a polarity of shape and color, but even they can only hint at the abundancy of color possible through breeding **Philodendrons**. These plants cannot really be called ever-"green" — very rarely are their leaves totally green (see picture on page 56). The **Philodendron erubescens** has dark green leaves which shimmer pink on the edges and dark red growing point (incidentally, the flowers are also red). In the case of the magnificent new cultivar "**Red Emerald**" only the tops of the leaves have remained green. In both plants the margins of the leaves are without incisions. The "**Emerald Queen**" resembles the "Red Emerald" except for its distinguishing light green color. Both are characterized by their relatively slow growth rate and the fact that they can easily be trained by pruning.

Philodendron panduraeforme, **Fiddle Leaf Plant**, again makes its appearance among collections of large plants, and

Our selection of plants

another member of this family well worth knowing is the climbing *Philodendron sodiroi*, whose leaves undergo magnificent color-changes as it reaches maturity.

Philodendron Tuxla is another familiar plant and can be found in any good catalogue for hydroponics.

As regards the general care of *Philodendrons,* along with *Monstera,* they will present no problems, provided they have a uniformly light (but not sunny) position and are not moved. They are one of the most satisfying plants for hydroponicists. The changes in the shape of the leaves which take place in older specimens are normal for these plants.

Philodendron scandens, the well known creeper, causes problems if grown in the same pot as another plant, which it will often deprive of space and food.

Every plant lover is happy to see the plants he is looking after bloom or even bear fruit, for these are signs that the plant is in top condition. *Ficus benjamina* has, because of its elegant appearance enjoyed an unimpaired popularity for a long time – especially for large hydroponic units. Recently, however, it has been challenged by **Ficus diversifolia**, the **Mistletoe Fig**, which has attractive olive-like fruit; these also provide the opportunity of studying the peculiarities of the so-called parthenocarpic plants. Larger members of the *Ficus* family, ranging from the original Rubber Tree, the *Ficus elastica* (**Indian Rubber Plant**) to the

Left, a *Ficus schrijveriana*. This plant has light-speckled leaves and a pink growing tip.

Right, a monumental display – the hydroponic units are concealed by marble and the pillar is camouflaged by *Ficus benjamina*. Other plants shown – Pandanus, Screw Pine; *Ficus pumila*, the Climbing Fig which will deprive other plants of their nutrients if grown in the same pot (TWL).

Our selection of plants

Ficus lyrata, the **Banjo** or **Fiddle-back Fig**, which is now somewhat out of fashion, have been used in hydroponics for many decades and with great success. Like the **Banjo Fig** they all need a good prune from time to time. New cultivars have variously colored variegated foliage. The red-brown **Australian Fig**, *Ficus rubiginosa*, is especially effective if grown as a branching bush. It is only the **Creeping Fig**, *Ficus pumila*,

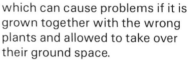

which can cause problems if it is grown together with the wrong plants and allowed to take over their ground space.

Hoya carnosa, also known as the **Wax Plant** or **Honey Plant**, is one of the oldest house-plants, already a favorite of our great grandmothers. It has successfully undergone the transformation to hydroponics. Just like its smaller relative *Hoya Bella*, the **Miniature Wax Plant**, with the dainty, hanging leaves and the more rapidly growing *Stephanotis floribunda*, **Madagascar Jasmine**.

These plants are evergreen climbers which flower abundantly in the summer. They are thus classed both as foliage and flowering plants, so why is it that people still criticize hydroponics for having a supposed miserable range of plants in the latter category? These three plants, for instance, have been producing magnificent flowers for many years now.

This *Hoya carnosa* 'variegata' was originally an unwanted ground creeper, accompanying another plant. Now it is a very decorative display in its own right.

Our selection of plants

Dizygotheca elegantissima, Finger Aralia, here growing on its own (cf. page 12).

Nephrolepsis exaltata ''Teddy Junior'', a cultivar of the Sword Fern family. It has grown into an enormous bush.

Leea rubra, a bushy plant from Java. At the moment it is not blooming, but it does have very interesting flowers.

Cycas revoluta, another new fern.

Our selection of plants

The **Hoya** and its above named relatives require a resting period during the winter, at a temperature of 10-15°C (50-59°F), and with a considerable reduction in the quantity of nutrient solution supplied. This is discussed in greater detail in the chapter on daily care. For this reason, however, it is far easier to keep the **Hoya carnosa ''variegata''** which will grow vigorously all year long, even if it does not flower. You must, however, separate it in time from unwelcome ''co-habitors'' and give it a pot of its own.

Dieffenbachia picta exotica and others are effective plants both on their own and in a group display. Their decorative value makes them indispensable in hydroponics. Remember, to maintain the beauty of their leaves, do not allow inflorescences to form.

As the author of this book repeatedly claims — hydroponics makes the best even of a bad situation. This picture provides the proof for her claim — this splendid collection of plants are growing next to a radiator, at a window which faces south. Middle right, a *Chlorophytum* 'tower' which is constructed of two paper baskets made of bark, which are placed one on top of the other. Some of the plants, such as the *Euphorbia lactea* on the left and the Somona are shown elsewhere in the book on their own.

To return to the Wax Plant. On page 71 there is a picture of a **Hoya Carnosa** which is obviously flourishing. In just over ten years it has grown into a magnificent wall creeper. The photograph being taken in April meant it had only developed one inflorescence — many more soon followed but, unfortunately, we needed the picture immediately.

On the page opposite you can see four less common plants — each one is a contradition to the claim that certain plants, for example ferns, cannot be grown hydroponically.

Our selection of plants

True flowering plants

And so we at last come to the "true" flowering plants. Of course, we have to admit to those who say they are not suitable for hydroponics, that these plants do indeed fail to fulfil the oft-repeated fundamental aim of hydro-ponics – for with the best of will they cannot be "beautiful all year round" like the evergreen *Cissus*, ivy, palms and other such plants.

The flowering of the plant is the climax of its development. This is as integral to the plant's growth rhythm as is the fact that, with very few exceptions, the time spent building up to flower formation and blooming is considerably greater than the climax itself.

There are very few plants which are an exception. Orchids grown hydroponically can keep their flowers in a reasonable condition for many weeks. The **African Violet** (see opposite) does have periods when it produces incredibly large numbers of magnificent flowers but it only stops flowering completely for a short while at the turn of the year. In my opinion, the most amazing of all is the succulent *Somona* "Gabriela". I have had this plant for 5 years and it has never been without its magnificent flowers.

Hibiscus rosa-sinensis, more commonly called the China Rose, provides excellent evidence that plants grown hydroponically can produce magnificent flowers. If you look carefully, you will even see that this little plant is producing a second flower bud. And it will continue to bloom every summer until it has grown into a little tree and is accommodated in a large bucket-like container.

These African Violets are perhaps my most amazing plants. Above, the African Violet which I propagated in 1963 from a leaf cutting. The photograph was taken in 1980. Unfortunately this ancient plant did not survive the attempt to transfer it into a modern hydroponic unit in 1982. Below, this African Violet was part of the plant discussed above, but it grew too heavy and broke off in the spring of 1978. Unexpectedly it took root again and I consequently call it a "vegetative twin". The photograph shown was taken in 1980. As with the old plant, it continues to flourish and flower, growing on two tuffs.

Our selection of plants

And now we come back to the Arum family. Their contribution to this section of plants is in no way exhausted by the non-flowering (or rarely flowering) plants such as *Dieffenbachia, Monstera* and *Philodendron* among others. In fact, no hydroponicist can possibly remain unfamiliar for any length of time with two of its flowering members in particular.

The *Spathiphyllum* **wallisii**, also called the **Peace Lily** (see picture page 54) is the best plant to use for group displays. It hardly exceeds 20-30cm (8-12in) in

This little Orange Tree, *Citrus mitis*, should not be forgotten. While the fruits are still ripening new flowers appear.

height, and even exudes — as I have been able to confirm repeatedly — a faint smell of violets from its everlasting inflorescences. As regards the durability of the beautiful, long-lasting snow-white "sails" it still has advantages over the more recent hybrids with their bigger bracts which, at worst, may even turn green. From April/May **S. wallisi** will also develop seeds from its first inflorescences. These germinate easily. Spathiphyllum should not be grown in the same pot as other plants and should, if this is the case, be transferred as soon as possible.

The *Anthurium scherzerianum*, the **Flamingo Flower**, can scarcely be surpassed — it has splendid leaves and flowers and also lives a long time. The "flowers" are, of course, as with all the Arum family, technically speaking inflorescences. They consist of the beautifully colored spathe which are really a greatly developed ornamental leaf (unlike the rosette of bracts of the **Poinsettia**, proper name *Euphorbia pulcherrima*) and the spadix which later also carries the seeds. In some Anthuriums the latter even tends to curl. Today we are dealing almost exclusively with cultivars. The plants with the most beautiful flowers are hybrids between

The Flamingo Flower, an *Anthurium-Andreanum* hybrid. It flowers easily and lives a long time. It is thus very suitable for hydroponics.

Anthurium andreanum, **Painter's Palette**, and **Anthurium scherzerianum.** The foliage of the latter is narrower than the long-stemmed shiny **Andreanum** leaves. Both hybrid groups prefer humid conditions during the main growth period from March onwards, constant warmth and light (but not direct sun) and should not be moved. The nutrient solution should always, even in the winter, have a temperature of about 18 °C (64 °F).

Bromeliads must not be omitted in any collection of hydroponically grown plants.

Above, *Vriesea splendens*, also called Flaming Sword. In this specimen the offset is still attached to the mother plant yet it has already produced a flower.

Below, *Aechmea fasciata*, the Greek Vase Plant, which is highly valued for its relative longevity. They are called Vase Plants because the leaves of the central rosette form a vaseline container at their base. This should be kept filled with a little water — occasionally adding a tiny amount of LEWATIT HD5 — until the end of the flower's and plant's growth period. Unlike with the LEWATIT, if you are following the traditional method for making up the nutrient solution added to the "vase", you must ensure the water hardness is not above 5°dH. The plant absorbs the water/weak nutrient solution with the aid of special cells at the base of the rosette.

Our selection of plants

However much you admire the **Bromeliads**, those brilliant exotic plants, it must be said, with regard to their short life span, they cannot really be classed as true hydroponic plants. Indirectly though, one could argue, they do not die — they live on through offsets which emerge from their roots while the flower is already slowly dying.

And I can confirm from my own experience that such an offset, when left attached to its mother-plant, a **Vriesea**, produced a specially beautifully colored "flaming sword" when it was no less than two years old. This is often the case in hydroponics.

Begonias are commonly divided into three major groups. The first includes the short-lived flowering Begonias which, being annuals, are not really suitable for our purposes. I did manage to keep an **Elatior Begonia** alive and flowering for 2½ years but this was a rare exception.

This *Dracaena fragrans lindenii* is standing in the author's study. In 1978 it came from Guatemala to Luxembourg as a small Ti Tree and it was there that she bought it. Unfortunately, it is now no longer variegated, having suffered a tissue disease, which it had probably acquired before its sale. However, since then, it has grown so well in hydroponics that it stands almost three metres (yards) above the top of the container.

Our selection of plants

This bush Begonia hybrid "Cleopatra" grows slowly and flowers abundantly. It is especially striking because the undersides of the leaves are dark red. It is very suitable for hydroponics.

In the second group of Begonias we can find the extremely hardy and readily flowering bushy types; some of these begin to flower when they are still very young indeed. If cut back carefully before their growth period, without however stripping them of their lower leaves, then they can live many years, especially in hydroponics if the roots are kept healthy. The third group is equally well-suited to hydroponics. This group consists of the foliage begonias whose leaves are astounding in their range of colors and shapes. The most famous of these begonias are the **Begonia Rex** hybrids. Over the years I have owned many of these plants, but my favourite was a **B. manicata** which came to me as a cutting from Switzerland in the mid-60's. Unfortunately I had to give it away because it grew too large, which was a pity but could not be helped.

These plants survive the winter well if they are placed in a moderately warm position, with a room temperature of about 15°C (59°F). The level of the nutrient solution should be reduced to 10mm (⅜in).

If you are using a deionizer then this reduction can be carried out

Our selection of plants

without any problems. However, in the case of the traditional method you have to first reduce the level of the nutrient solution by half since a reduction of the water-level alone would result in a proportionate increase of the salt content. This is dangerous and can even be fatal for the roots. This is of course true for all house-plants, and not just Begonias, which are in a similar situation. Since there are also Begonias which grow outdoors the following should be noted. Foliage and bush begonias are of tropical origin; they must be kept indoors all year round.

The **Wax Plant** has already been discussed on page 60, but there we were concerned with the variegated, flowerless *Hoya carnosa variegata.* In the picture opposite, however, we have a perfect example of the original species of *Hoya carnosa,* which has beautifully scented flowers from mid-May right into the late autumn when it is still warm. If placed in the right conditions it should not be moved all year, nor should it be turned. This plant can grow very old indeed.

This giant Wax Plant *Hoya carnosa* is already very many years old. Unfortunately, whenever its photograph is taken, it still has not started flowering, so all you can see is its foliage.

Our selection

The much loved cacti

Almost everybody knows that cacti are among the most popular house-plants, yet not every hydroponicist has turned his attention to these plants. For again and again we find hydroponicists who shake their heads in disbelief when they are told by others, who have long devoted themselves almost exclusively to cacti, that no plants could be more perfect for hydroponics than the cacti family and other succulents. The following reservation must, however, be made – their success depends on being able to regulate the water-level with

Echinocereus grusonii, the famous Golden Barrel, photographed in April, 1981. Height from the top of the container = 42 cm (17 in), diameter at top (including spines) = 104 cm (42 in). Here it is still in the same container as in the picture above, taken in 1965. Since being photographed here it has been transferred to a "small large" container with a 2 litre (½ gallon) installable tank and is doing well.

Taken in 1965, this picture shows an assortment of cacti. Far left, *Echinocereus grusonii,* which at that time was about ten years old and just transferred to a brand new ceramic container from the SOMBRERO series. You can also see various large Opuntias, succulent Euphorbias, a flowering Crown of Thorns and several other small cacti. It is obvious from this picture that the pioneers of hydrophonics also knew that cacti and other succulents were ideal for hydroponics, provided they were treated correctly.

Our selection of plants

This grafted *Cleistocactus wendlandii* has grown six offsets. Foreground, a small Optunia in a mini HYDRO-TANK.

Euphorbia grandicornis can all too easily be confused for a cactus.

great precision. If the water-level is kept too high, or even worse, reaches the necks of the roots which are so sensitive to water, then all succulents will die. The **Golden Barrel (*Echinocereus grusonii*)** shown on page 72 is now about 25 years old and has obviously not fallen victim to such errors. Its shape has, however, suffered somewhat and not developed to a true "golden barrel", because nobody dared transplant it in time. The ***Wendlandii Cleistocactus*** with its six offshoots could also do better. It was grown without being grafted and as a result will not produce its first flowers for a long time. But such finer points are usually not discovered until it is too late. Still, the cactus does have three new shoots. Incidentally, as of old, only liquid concentrate should be used for making the nutrient solution according to the traditional method. We have luckily left behind the age of tablets and powders.

Our selection

There is a world of difference between "true" cacti and the jointed and leafed kinds.

Whether we are referring to the **Christmas** or **Easter cacti** or to the large hybrids known as *Phyllocactus,* they all prove that those grown hydroponically and looked after properly produce a greater richness of flowers, both in quantity and in color, than their traditionally grown potted counterparts, however excellent these may be. It is not without reason that the large Epiphyllens, which bloom in the late summer, have been called "orchid cacti". Their flowers really are amazing.

Rhipsalidopsis gaertheri, the pink Easter Cactus, will flower reliably for years on end, just like its relative the Christmas Cactus.

Epiphyllum ackermannii, an old cultivar of Mexican leaf cacti, is as magnificent as the Christmas and Easter Cacti.

Our selection

The "other" succulents

The three-year-old *Beaucarnea recurvata* shown above, while still a so-called seeding, looks just like a bulb. No one would imagine it could develop into a Pony Tail Plant (see picture opposite).

The older the *Beaucarnea recurvata,* the more grotesque its shape. This plant can grow to a very large size, thus becoming increasingly expensive and valuable. In addition to its high decorative value, it is ideal as regards ease of care, both qualities being due to the distorted trunk. Originally bulbous, and it is from here the "pony tail" grows, its trunk becomes more unshapely, acting as a water store. It can supply the plant with moisture for months on end, even if standing in direct sunlight. As the plant increases in size, its growth rate decreases.

Often still sold as *Nolina recurvata* it was also once thought to belong to the Lily family. Now it is classified as an *Agavaceae.*

A variegated Wax Flower is sharing the same pot (cf. page 60).

Our selection

There is a very impressive example of these "other" succulents at the start of this section (see previous two pages). Succulents belong to various different plant families and thus surprising inter-relationships can arise. Even where we least expect it, we find that some of the most common houseplants have

succulent sub-divisions. From these you can take any example and you will have an extraordinary plant which positively flourishes in hydroponics.

Beaucarnea recurvata (see page 76/7) perfectly illustrates the strangeness of form and unproblematic nature that characterizes these plants. I do, however, feel slightly uneasy citing this particular plant as an example. Although the one shown here is a legitimately reared specimen of this strange Mexican Agavaceae family, certain enormous, expensive examples quite justifiably angered some people at the German National Horticultural Show in Kassel, 1981, because they had clearly been standing

Above, *Euphorbia tirucalli,* the Milk Bush, which has bushy, leafless stems. Below, *Euphorbia lactea,* with its white stripe up the middle.

Our selection of plants

for decades in Mexico before they somewhat illegally suddenly appeared on sale and at exhibitions in Germany. These were "veteran" plants which, without any consideration for conservation, had been kidnapped from their native land. Luckily I can watch my modest **Pony Tail Plant** grow without a guilty conscience. These plants are still rarities in Europe, but are very popular in the United States.

But to return to the subject of "other" succulents. First of all it must be noted that they are in no way related to the large family of cacti. It is only because they share the characteristic of being adapted to retain water (i.e., are "succulents") and because they physically resemble one another, that confusion arises. For example, the several hundred kinds of succulents known as **Euphorbiae** or more commonly the Spurge family have mistakingly been called "Cacti of the Old World" whereas it is a fact that all true cacti—with the exception of the leaf cacti—come from the deserts of the New World. The differences are

Above, *Somona*, "Gabriela" a natural hybrid of the Crown of Thorns from Madagascar.
Below, *Crassula arborea*, a very hardy *Crassulaceae*.

Our selection of plants

Pachypodium lamerei, the familiar Madagascar Palm with a very unusual "crest" or crista.

milky juice which is poisonous to varying degrees. This property, which is shared by the succulents ***Apocynaceae*** whose poison is often fatal, has to a large extent been responsible for their rapid increase in the wild. To ascertain whether your plant(s) contain(s) this juice, just scratch the surface of the leaf with a needle. This knowledge might be to your advantage. The charming **Somona** is also a true Euphorbia, including its small (12-15cm (5-6 in) in height permanently flowering varieties. If you are aware of this fact and treat these plants accordingly,

Kalanchoe beharensis, Velvet Leaf, belongs to the harmless family of *Crassulaceae.* It has strikingly beautiful velvet leaves.

obvious when you compare the flowers. But how does the hydroponicist go about classifying his ***Euphorbia lactea*** if he does not know its name? Just like the European Spurges, the garden **"Snow on the Mountain", "Crown of Thorns (E. milii)** and **Poinsettia**, the tropical variety also contain a

Adenium obesum, the Desert Rose, is a Pachypodium which, through being grafted on Oleander has lost its thick stem, and now flowers even more magnificently. The specimen in the picture is growing in a medium-sized HYDRO-TANK, standing on a table. It is already several years old and bears 40 flowers.

you will be highly satisfied with their progress in hydroponic units – as is the case with all succulents. The flowers of the **Somona** all require a lot of light. The *Pachypodiae* (see above and page 80) are close relatives of the Oleander and, would you believe it, of the evergreen **Vinca major.** When still developing they may resemble a heavily thorned version of the column cactus – right up to their crown of leaves. The *Pachypodium lameri,* the Madagascar Palm (see top, page 80) whose highly scented flowers do not appear until the plant is quite old,

clearly illustrates what I mean. Did you know that in south-west Africa you can find over a dozen beautifully flowering succulents belonging to the Geranium family? Or that along with *Cissus antarctica,* the **Kangaroo Vine,** and its more delicate cultivar "**Ellen Danica**" there is also a *Cissus cactiformis* which hangs down like a smooth cactus. And how about this – my **Cape Ivy** (see page 46) bears little yellow flowers which look like tiny sunflowers and yet, belongs to the family of Compositae genus *Senecio.*

Our selection of plants

Bulbs

The success of flowering bulbs in hydroponics has, for me, always been a self-evident truth. So much so, that I feel I do not really need to waste many words on the subject. I was thus totally astounded when I read that **Amaryllis** is "not a suitable plant for hydroponics". This is simply not true, provided you remember that their natural growth cycle must not be contradicted (as with all flowering plants) and that bulbs are highly sensitive to too much water. They do also require a constant warmth of about 25°C (77°F) for forcing – but again this is nothing unusual. I set my first bulbs around Christmas and then at regular intervals, with the result that I have superb flowers continuously right into May. After flowering, the plants require very little care until August, when I put them aside for their resting period. They should be stored at a

temperature of about 10°C (50°F) and with only a tiny trace of moisture.

If bulbs fail to do well indoors — be they in earth or in a hydroponic unit — or if they do not flower again, then it is usually because they have not been looked after properly, either during or after flowering. Also, the bulbs may not have had sufficient warmth during the resting period. My oldest Amaryllis is now 15 years old; the bulb this year (before

Right, "Frühzauber" is the name given to this Amaryllis hybrid from South Africa. It begins flowering early, in November. This specimen has grown very well indeed.

Left, this *Hippeastrum* cultivar "Happy Memory" was bred by the Dutch Amaryllis specialist Ludwig.

This snow white beauty was originally grown in soil and transferred to hydroponics in 1976. It now flowers regularly every autumn and spring.

producing shoots) measures 44cm (18in) in diameter!

Our selection of plants

Orchids – for specialists only?

Whatever the method of cultivation, this question will come up again and again, but there is nevertheless a clear upward trend in the orchid's popularity; this popularization does not, however, impair its high standing in the plant world in any way. It is well known that we too have been trying for years to secure a place for these magnificent flowers in hydroponics.

The delightful **Paphiopedilum**, *the* **Slipper Orchid**, *and its different varieties, proved to be very suitable for hydroponics and bloomed again and again over the years.*

It could be that, as a terrestrial orchid (i.e. those which grow in the ground) it was naturally more disposed to hydroponics than the epiphytic kind (those which grow on trees). The latter, even when great care was taken and all the rules followed, did not grow successfully; being used to a ventilated, moist rather than wet growing medium, their roots are highly sensitive to even the slightest contact with the nutrient solution.
The strong white roots of the

Phalaenopsis or **Moth Orchid** when grown in a unit with a constant low water-level of 5mm (¼ in), always grew exactly on the water/air boundary whereas the fine root hairs remained in the moist air and between the equally moist air of the expanded clay granules. The result can be seen in the pictures on the opposite page – superb flowers developed as did four large foliage leaves and aerial roots. New flower buds even appeared. These results were repeated at an orchid farm and by several particularly knowledgeable orchid growers.
There really is a good reason why *Phalaenopsis* was chosen as an example. Although once said to be highly delicate, it has now been much perfected through breeding and can be regarded as the best of the

These three pictures show the development of a Phalaenopsis hybrid. It is growing in a HYDRO-TANK S, and it was easy to maintain the necessary constant low water-level. It has 18 flower buds on 3 stalks. In the last week its development was as follows –
Phase 1 (top left) 4 flowers, 14 buds.
Phase 2 (top right) 8 flowers, 10 buds.
Phase 3 (bottom) full bloom – 18 beautiful, fully opened flowers. These lasted many weeks. It is interesting to note that this orchid is supposedly very prone to losing its buds!
Since this photograph was taken the plant has flowered equally magnificently on two further occasions.

Our selection of plants

epiphytic orchids for growing at home. To promote better aeration of the roots it is often grown in an orchid basket using plant matter, either **Osmunda** (the roots of the **Regal Fern** or **Sphagnum Moss**) as a growing medium. This, being organic, is decomposable, and thus the orchid has to be transplanted frequently. Growing the plant hydroponically is therefore of great advantage.

Using expanded clay granules, which are inorganic and thus do not decompose, means the plant does not need to be transplanted for many years.

Odontoglossum grande, Tiger Orchid. It flowers from autumn onwards and grows well in hydroponics.

In addition the low water-level can be regulated very precisely. Please note that the additional and individual requirements for looking after orchids must also be met. This is not, however, the place to go into this subject.
For my own part, I have tried out a whole list of orchids which are supposed to do well indoors in my hydroponic units.
The next best specimen after my **Phalaenopsis** and **Paphiopedilum** was a **Odontoglossum,** otherwise called **Tiger Orchid**. This has always been a firm favorite among enthusiasts because of its high decorative value and relative ease of care. But it will die even in the hands of an expert if it is not allowed to rest once it has finished blooming in autumn/late autumn.
If you have seriously become obsessed with orchid-growing then you will not progress unless you consult specialist books and get together with other like-minded growers. Also you should not set your aims too high. I also found that **Coelogyne cristata, Cymbidium** hybrids and **Lycaste aromatica** did well, but **Cattleya** hybrids are not advisable for beginners and even my **Dendrobium thyrsiflorum,** after flowering twice, remained but a fond memory.

Our selection of plants

Other plants suitable for hydroponics

(B. = for beginners)

Abutilon, **Flowering Maple:** Winter 12–15 °C, prune in spring.

Agave & Aloe: as for cacti and other succulents.

Aglaonema, **Chinese Evergreen** & others: Aracae fam. as Dieffenbachia, see page 123.

Asparagus densiflorus,

Asparagus Fern *(A. sprengeri)*,

A. falcatus & *A. Scandens*. (All B.)

Aspidistra eliator, **Cast Iron Plant;** requires a lot of nutrients otherwise no problems. (B.)

Clivia miniata, **Kaffir Lily;** requires strict resting period.

Cordyline terminalis, **Flaming Dragon Tree:** as for Dracaenae.

Cryptanthus, **Starfish Plant:** Bromeliae. Harmless to grow in same pot as other plants. Some species flower easily.

Filicatae, **Ferns:** *Adiantum* **(Maidenhair Fern),** *Asplenium nidus* **(Bird's Nest Fern),** *Platycerium* **(Stag's Horn Fern),** etc. For warm, moderate rooms. See *Nephrolepsis* 'Teddy Junior', page 61.

Guzmania: see *Bromeliae*.

Gynura aurantiaca, **Purple Passion Vine** or **Velvet Plant:** velvet, purple leaves; hanging plant. (B.)

Haemanthus albiflos, **Blood Lily:** evergreen. (B.)

Hedera helix, **Common Ivy:** cool resting period indispensable.

Kalanchoe daigremontianum, **Good Luck Plant** *(Bryophyllum):* succulents.

Maranta, **Prayer Plant:** good on own or in same pot with other plant.

Nerium oleander: cuttings easy to propogate; young plants good but later too big.

Nidularium, **Bird's Nest:** see *Bromeliae*, page 68.

Palmae, **Palms — Areca, Betel Nut Palm,** *Kentia*, *Washingtonia:* all good.

Pandanus veitchii, **Screw Pine:** well suited; later develops very attractive aerial roots, see page 2.

Peperomia, **Pepper Elder;** good.

Pilea cadieri, **Aluminium Plant:** variegated, upright. **P. microphylla (Artillery Plant)** good ground creeper.

Sansevviera trifasciata laurentii, **Mother-in-Law's Tongue:** standard plant, will flower easily, attractive cultivars.

Schefflera actinophylla, **Umbrella Tree:** evergreen, large variety. In winter, when heated, susceptible to pests. Today also small varieties, better — eg. *S. aboricola*.

Setcreasea purpurea, **Purple Heart:** as for Tradescantiae. Frequent offsets.

Sprekelia formosissima, **Aztec Lily:** resting period November–March; otherwise as for Amaryllis.

Stapelia, **Carrion Flower:** succulent relative of **Wax Plant;** interesting flower in summer.

Streptocarpus hybridus, **Cape Primrose:** hybrids recently 'discovered' in hydroponics.

Tradescantiae: various species many of which flower easily (B.); frequent offsets.

Zantedeschia aethiopica, **White Calla Lily:** as for Amaryllis only with different growth rhythm. White flowers.

Zebrina pendula, **Wandering Jew:** colored leaves. As for Tradescantiae, only more light and warmth. (B.)

Looking after your plants

It is inevitable that in this chapter we shall have to recapitulate to a certain extent that which makes hydroponics such a viable long-term method of growing and caring for your plants. After all hydroponics does boast the longevity of its plants and the fact that they are easy to look after because they do not require constant attention. It must of course be said that there have always been potted plants which have lasted a long time, but, on the whole, plants grown in earth have not acquired the overall reputation for longevity that is associated with hydroponics. Perhaps partly because many potted plants are annuals and are intended to be thrown away after one year.

However, to do justice to hydroponic's purpose, you have to be familiar with all the prerequisites and practical measures which will ensure your plant's potential long life.

For only then will you profit from the advantages of this soilless cultivation and thus also make initial expenses really worth their while.

Whatever equipment and accessories you buy will, however, last a long time, whether it is a humidifier or a

Left, this *Elatior* Begonia turned out not to be an annual like many of these Begonias when grown in soil. As I already commented on page 69, it must obviously have been provided with optimal conditions for the 2½ years of its life.
Right, a monumental arrangement of 2 large hexagonal units. The variety of the plant heights has a particularly decorative and impressive effect. The *Dracaena fragrans massangeana* trees have all been carefully selected for their regular growth and straight stems. The height differences range from 50 to 150 cms (20 to 60 in). Two shrubby specimens also serve as "camouflage" for the surface of expanded clay in the containers. This function is complemented by the careful arrangement of *Scindapsus aureus*. The whole group is elegant and practical – a rare combination. (OTTO Hydropflanzen).

Looking after your plants

special light. Even the containers and expanded clay granules can be used again and again — of course, only after the necessary cleaning. But do not use chemical household cleaners or dish washing liquids. Hot water and, at the most, a quick scrub with pure soap will adequately clean any pot which has no cracks or chips. You can "boil" the expanded clay granules to disinfect them totally, but it usually suffices to swill them off thoroughly with hot water.

If you have even the slightest suspicion that the previous plant may have died due to infection or rot, then you will only add to your losses if you re-use either the pot or the expanded clay granules.

In this case the same precautions apply as if the plant were grown in soil — it is better to use totally new materials. And, because it is such an important point, let me remind you again of the dangers of wooden or bamboo sticks as supports for your plants — unfortunately a common occurrence even at reputable nurseries. See pages 26 and 27, text and pictures, as a reminder. On the opposite page is another sad warning (see picture).

It is true that you cannot always buy small supports for plants which are made of plastic or glass fibre and will not rot. And naturally, when the plant is still in the nurseries it is usually too early to recognize any signs of root rot. Usually the damage does not manifest itself until a few months later and this mistake, so often overlooked, will be the buyer's loss. He may well wonder why, whenever he tests the nutrient solution with MERCKOQUANT strips, the nitrate level is dangerously high. Everything however soon becomes clear when he decides to untie the flower sticks or bamboo cane to pull them out for a check. The foul smell that follows reveals the presence of rot, which is further confirmed by the appearance of the supports themselves (see picture opposite).

To protect the buyer, plants grown hydroponically which are supported either by wooden sticks or by bamboo canes should by rights be denied a seal of good quality.

But the buyer himself could refuse to buy such plants and should expect the supports to be resistant to the nutrient solution, as is the case with all the pots and containers suitable

Looking after your plants

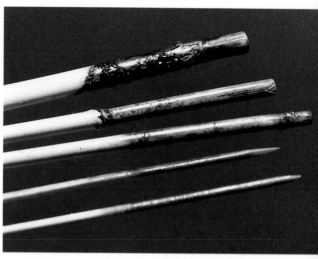

These wooden and bamboo supports have rotted through contact with the nutrient solution. The top cane was almost responsible for the death of a *Philodendron;* it only took one year for the damage to be done. The brown stained tips of the other supports also signify dangerous rot.

for hydroponics.
But this is not the only problem where the origins lie in the plant's past. Hothouses and flower shops also conceal many dangers.

You have to pay as much attention to where you buy your plants as to what you actually choose.

Some travelling salesmen, market stalls and so forth may sell "bargains" which, after a few days, prove to be normal potted plants just crudely transferred to hydroponic containers; they might even still have a ball of soil surrounding their roots, which is simply concealed by a layer of expanded clay granules.

But problems may still arise even if the plant has been expertly reared before its sale.

If the latticed nursery pot is too small, then, as the plant's growth rate suddenly increases, the constricted roots will turn into a veritable jungle.

I have come across examples in which the only means of giving the pot-bound roots room to grow, was to carefully cut open the nursery pot and remove the plant. To avoid this danger some nurseries use SCHLITZI, a white polystyrene nursery pot with fracture lines (see picture page 18). When the roots require more space, the pot breaks along these weak points.

Looking after your plants

Some seedlings are forced on special growing mediums such as GRODAN or rock wool. Initially they do well but later they are permanently kept wrapped in a wet "bandage", which is bad for most roots and promotes rot. In good hydroponic nurseries these special growing mediums are carefully removed before the plant is transferred to the container in which it is sold. In the case of home nurseries it is better to avoid these mediums from the very start — this can save a lot of trouble. For further details on home care see page 106ff.

The main points on pots and containers have already been made in a separate chapter concentrating on this one subject (see page 18ff).

Again I have to expressly warn against growing too many plants in one unit and against buying pots which are too small for the growing plant.

Do, however, remember that slow-growing cacti and certain succulents will require less room. In all other cases the 11cm (4in) pot is invariably too small for long-term purposes and the 15cm (6in) pot should really be the minimum size used.

The Amaryllis shown below spent four years in a 11 cm (4 in) pot which was far too small for it. When the pot was cut open, the severe constriction forced upon the roots was patently obvious.

Looking after your plants

To repeat a familiar point — in the case of plants grown in soil you must always carefully observe the specifications given as regards the size of the pot to be used. In hydroponics, however, it is really a case of 'the bigger the better'.

If you are solely concerned with the decorative effect of your plants then perhaps you will object to this on aesthetic grounds. But surely expanded clay granules are not an unattractive surface covering? The narrower the container the higher the requisite water-level for long-term care. We have however learned that optimum growth conditions require a constant, low water-level and that the plant should be spared continuous fluctuations of high/low levels. So table units should at least be wide at the bottom so that they can hold more water at a low level. Otherwise you will have to continuously supply tiny quantities of water in order that the roots are not deprived of water or breathing space. *This, however, abnegates the very purpose of hydroponics.*

The roots, having been carefully arranged on a layer of expanded clay, are then gradually covered up with more of the granules. Throughout this process slowly rotate the pot (cf. transference).

By gently shaking the plant, you can position the bulb correctly. Repotted in April, the plant can then develop its full foliage over the summer; the resting period in the winter should be ignored.

Looking after your plants

Water — a problematic question

At this point I would strongly recommend you to turn back to page 40 and reread the chapter titled "From water to nutrient solution" to remind yourself of the principal recurring problems. In doing so the previous section on the size of pots and containers will also be further illuminated. I would also like to quote from a highly competent source that *95% of all problems in hydroponics are the result of incorrect "watering".*

Although this percentage is an example of hyperbole and we do know that there are other equally serious errors which cannot simply be blamed on "water-happy" hydroponicists, this statement is on the whole correct. Watering is also a major problem when growing plants in soil. Instead of paying attention to the rise and fall in the plant's water requirements, which vary according to the time of year, people continue to water like mad, convinced that the plants must not go thirsty! They do not understand or even consider that the roots might thereby be deprived of air to breathe and the plant is quite simply drowned. The next chapter will deal with the use of the HYDRO-TANK.

This unit, thanks to its special reservoir, allows the plant to draw only the water it needs and thus maintains a strictly regulated low water-level. But before we come to this topic, there are still a few more points to be made.

All water which is used for your plants must be at room temperature.

This rule applies to all hydroponicists, whether they use LEWATIT HD5 or follow the traditional method. Never ever use water directly from the cold tap — this will chill and damage your plants. The term "at room temperature" is as imprecise as "lukewarm" or "hand-hot" so you will need a suitable thermometer to test that your water has a temperature of 22-24°C (72-75°F) before you use it.

If following the traditional method then you should also only add fresh water in strict proportion to the amount used, for the nutrient solution and the added water cannot remain indefinitely in the holder. Concerning the frequency and amount required, you will have to follow your own judgment. It may be useful to use the following as a guideline: when the float goes down to

Looking after your plants

Minimum, top up the nutrient solution with fresh water, but only with 3 weeks' supply.

After 2, or at the most 3 weeks, the float should again be indicating Minimum and that more water is required.

If consumption is higher you may add fresh water at any time — remember, not cold water! In the case of water-retentive plants such as cacti and succulents, this "refill-dosage" will be decreased as necessary. This whole procedure may at first seem very inconvenient, but it is in keeping with our original observation on water requirements.

In hydroponics you may often think your plants do not have enough water but in fact they may already have been given too much.

But please note — the above rules about topping up every 3 weeks instead of constantly flooding the plant out of the goodness of your heart, applies only to those who practise the traditional method of hydroponics and to those who have holders with water-level indicators. During the plant's maximum growth period, the nutrient solution has to be changed at about every 6-8 weeks. Here you should follow the instructions that accompany your particular nutrient preparation although there are again some general rules to be observed. This is especially important if you are going to make allowances for the seasonal changes and the resting period; but even plants which spend the winter in a heated room without a true resting period, still suffer from the decrease in daylight.

Always remember — the less light and warmth the plant receives, the less the quantities of nutrients and water it requires.

It suffices to rinse out the salt residues or previous nutrient solutions and to keep the water-level so low that the roots are only just moistened. This applies to a plant standing in average light conditions at a temperature of 10-12 °C (50-58 °F). It is highly advisable to check the water-level from time to time and to moisten with slightly warm water when necessary.
Hydroponically grown plants rarely dry out, but if they do it is almost invariably the owner's fault and another cultural error.

Looking after your plants

More simply — LEWATIT HD5

So far we have dealt almost exclusively with the traditional method when discussing the subject of water — now it is time to consider the deionizer LEWATIT HD5. Using liquid concentrate or powder to make up the required nutrient solution and changing it every 2 months is all well and good. It is efficient and, not taking into account the additional time spent, cheap. I have myself worked with this method long enough and thus am speaking from experience.

But LEWATIT HD5 has truly revolutionized modern hydroponics and become indispensable.

Admittedly it is more expensive to buy, whether in small, ready-packed quantities or on a larger scale intended for self-mixing. If however you take into account the great saving as regards time and effort expended and that the nutrient solution will only need totting up about every 6 months, then this expense is soon cancelled out.

It is also better for the plant if you can leave it without disturbance for long periods of time.

Now you can avoid the often laborious routine of carrying the plant around, removing the pot from the holder (which means running the risk of root damage) and frequently rinsing and cleaning the container.
It is advisable to return to the chapter on nutrition (page 40ff.) to remind yourself of the requirements given for the use of LEWATIT HD5. You will then also remember that LEWATIT HD5 is also available in small packets (see picture page 45). These are like tea-bags — you just immerse them in the water — and have superseded the old-fashioned, inconvenient nutrient batteries, which had to be jammed in the base of the inner pot. To exchange them you simply have to remove them from the container and this need only be done every 6 months. BAYER'S original tins of loose LEWATIT HD5 are intended for sprinkling onto the expanded clay granules. They then have to be rinsed through the growing medium with water. It goes without saying that in doing so (a) too much water may be used and (b) too large a quantity of used LEWATIT may accumulate in the plant roots, especially in the case of small pots and those with few openings. However, this may still be the lesser evil when you think of the frequent

Looking after your plants

removal of the plant from its holder involved in the traditional method.

Pruning

The photograph below shows a plant with incredibly pot-bound roots and raises the question of pruning. Can you get a plant back "into shape" by pruning both the roots and/or the foliage? This is indeed the answer to the problem and hydoponically grown plants are no different here from any other plant which can be cut back. Pruning works best for *Ficus benjamina* and other **Rubber Trees**, *Philodendrons*, and *Schefflera*. Normal trimming of shoots and thinning out of bare branches can be carried out on a wide range of plants — as in the case of plants potted in soil. The most suitable time for trimming and pruning your plants is during the spring/early summer.

At this time in particular, controlled pruning and stopping can greatly stimulate growth.

It is said that root growth can be curbed by decreasing the plant's nutrients whereas, in fact, it has the inverse effect. If the plant is "hungry" then root development increases so that the roots can search for more food. In addition, a "hungry" plant will in the long run be weakened and be susceptible to pests.

Looking after your plants

Wintercare

Beginners should not choose plants which demand complicated attention during their resting period, but concentrate instead on those which are recommended as being easy to care for in the winter and well-adapted to life indoors all year round. Maintaining a low water-level, which is today usually considered a 'must', helps the plants to save energy and survive even if the temperature is somewhat lower. The choice of "easy-care" plants is sufficiently wide — ranging from Palms to Philodendrons to African Violets. It is also very important to avoid placing the hydroponic units — especially the larger ones — on stone floors. This inevitably promotes the dreaded "cold feet" if the level of the cold nutrient solution is also too high. A 20mm (¾ in) Styropor tile would already remedy the situation. Such a tile is also ideal for insulating the plant against higher temperatures if it is standing on a window sill or a heater.

New instruments are constantly being brought out for heating individual plants. Left, "electric blankets" by Bayer; middle, heating apparatus with a probe by DANFORD; top left, hot plate by KRIEGER; bottom left, FLORATHERM cable.

My fitted window-ledge heating system, with heating cables and a thermostatic control to make individual adjustments. This system has worked effectively and reliably for many years.

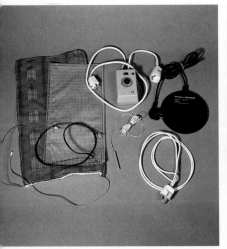

Looking after your plants

The humidity of the air also plays an important role in the well-being of your plant.

Nothing could be worse for a plant that is kept in a heated room than an overdry atmosphere. If in addition the light conditions are bad — which to a certain extent is unavoidable in the winter — and the plant has "cold feet", then the plant is very prone to attack by pests, which would usually not attack a healthy plant (see 'Plant protection — a must', page 116ff.).

N.B. — Of all the measures to be taken during the winter, the most important is to pay attention to the temperature of the water you use for your plant.

Whether you are using a hydrostatically regulated humidifier, which works according to condensation, or a manual mist spray, it is preferable to moisten the plant only in the late afternoon and, in the case of the spray, to use soft water — remember that this must be temperate. Using soft water avoids calcium spots being left on the leaves. Of course, you must always avoid direct, strong sunlight.
Plants from the tropical rain forests, for example

Philodendrons, are happiest in the winter at a humidity level of **50-60%**. Cacti and other succulents have "dry" resting periods in the winter and can, as recently confirmed in hydroponics, remain in the same place all year round.

A modern humidifier should be as unproblematic as possible. This one by BRUNE, model B110, works by condensation.

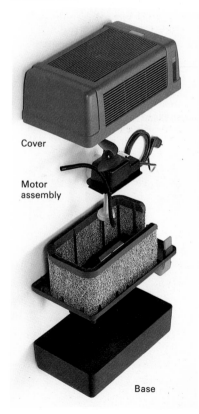

Cover

Motor assembly

Base

Looking after your plants

Natural and artificial light

Hydroponically grown plants, depending on their country of origin, need as much light as their potted equivalents.

Individual requirements may vary, hence my advice earlier that you should choose your plants according to the conditions you can provide and to group them with care. But remember that Man's eyes are so adaptable to different light conditions that they are the

The FLORASIX light meter by GOSSEN is highly reliable and made by a reputable firm. To read the measurements on the scale you simply hold the meter horizontally into the light.

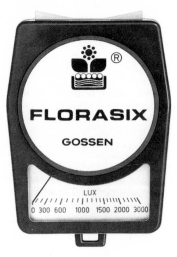

worst possible instruments for objectively judging what is bright, medium and bad light. Since light is all important for a plant — it cannot survive, never mind flourish, without the correct amount — it is essential that the plant's requirements are met to the full.

For this reason you will almost certainly need a reliable lightmeter.

At the moment I actually own five. One is an expensive instrument for professionals which, among other thing, allows me to check out the "cheap" instruments which are at present on the market. These do not seem to be very light sensitive; in semi-darkness they fail to distinguish all values below 100 lux. As far as I am concerned, however cheap they are, they are a total waste of money — never mind the damage they can cause if you trust their readings. It would then have been far cheaper to have spent a bit more in the very beginning.

For my own use I possess a FLORASIX (see picture opposite). Another warning though. It is usual that the measuring tables that come with these meters only provide the minimum light requirements

Looking after your plants

that a plant needs just to live. This may be somewhat confusing for the layman. The home grower can only conveniently sort his plants into groups and for each of these groups — ranging from high to low light requirements — work out an average.

This average fluctuates between 1,000-2,000 lux, which is the most suitable reading and also applies to artificial light conditions.

With the aid of a meter you can verify that weeks of overcast weather does indeed damage your plants. Flowers and colored leaves are especially vulnerable. Even in these days of energy conservation, we are able to counter these setbacks. OSRAM has developed special lights called FLORA SET, which use only a minimal amount of electricity and yet provide a high intensity light source which is unaccompanied by heat production. The area covered is also quite large.

Through experience I have learned that when the readings on the light meter indicate a deficiency, such artificial lighting can be used with great success, both as a complement to sunlight or as a replacement, burning 12 hours a day. The

FLORA-SET is the latest in artificial lighting for plants. It is easy to assemble and if properly adjusted can also be used for ground creepers.

requirements of creepers can also be met if the lights are positioned appropriately. These lights have such a long cable stored in their side, that the height at which they hang can be adjusted in proportion to the area you wish to be supplied with light.

Using the new HYDRO-TANK

The main characteristics

1. No water-level indicator. Instead you can see how much water is required by pressing on the lid of the table unit which then tips, or by removing the lid of the installable tank unit. In both cases the tank is revealed and this being transparent you can easily see the level of the water.

2. Once the base of the container has been filled with tepid water as required, then only cold water need be used for further topping up. This can be done at any time.

3. The inner pot is simply fitted into its special 'slot' and after that does not need to be moved or turned. This removes the risk of root damage.

4. Using a deionizer is, as expected, extremely convenient. Just drop the "tea-bag" into the container, near the tank. If using LEWATIT HD5 in its loose form, then always put these into the base of the container and never on the expanded clay granules, since here it would not be in contact with the water.

5. If following the traditional method then fill the base with tepid water as required when you first use the unit. The first tankful, especially in the case of plants recently transferred to hydroponics, should only contain clear water. You should not

Fill the tank to the brim

Quickly turn the tank through 180° so that the opening is at the bottom.

Adjust the water-level on the scale.

add any nutrient. This is also advisable if the plants have just come from a nursery – it helps them acclimatize. Later, alternate the supply in the tank between clear water and nutrient solution. Slight 'overdosages' in either direction are inevitable but are of no significance.

6. The advantages of this new design are by no means restricted to the rotatable tank ensuring a constant low water-level. There is a lot more to be said in its favor.

Here the dangers of growing two plants in the same pot are avoided, yet the Areca Palm and Ficus pumila are still in the same container and provided for by the same tank. (1 litre (quart) installable HYDRO-TANK).

The HYDRO-TANK 'S'

When it was discovered that the roots of some plants needed moist air but were also very sensitive to water, the HYDRO-TANK was re-designed to meet these requirements. By lowering the height of the axle bearings, the HYDRO-TANK 'S' (= Special) was developed. This new unit can justifiably be regarded as the ultimate in low water-level maintenance.

If the control is set on zero then there will only be a tiny amount of water released, yet this is more than enough for some plants during their resting period. This new unit has even meant that orchids, which often fail to flower, can be provided with optimal conditions and consequently flourish.

Using the new HYDRO-TANK

Nursery units with a tank

The constant low water-level of the 'S'-Tank, which apart from its success with orchids, has also proved ideal for cacti and other succulents and even ferns, has not been the only improvement in hydroponics due to Dr, Blaicher's new HYDRO-TANK. Innovations have also been possible in the nursery as a result of the new application of the 1 litre (1 quart) installable tank unit.

Instead of being fitted into a hydroponic unit, the rotatable tank and its brown container was placed on flat nursery trays of different sizes.

The question raised was whether the installable 1 litre tank (1 quart) could be used on its own help the small-scale greenhouse grower.

This would put an end to the watering routine and, in addition, growth would be even better due to the constancy of the water-level.

This was the general idea. The three-month experiment produced excellent results. Needlessly to say the experiments did not stop at nursery care. The set on page 107 was also developed, not only being used for the cacti-garden mentioned there, but also for mini tomato plants. In the large tray shown opp. I grew lettuce, chervil, dill and Pimpinella, maintaining a

These runner beans have been grown from the start in a large hydroponic container with a fitted 2 litre (½ gallon) tank. Previously they had always to be kept carefully drained, even when they were still seedlings. Clearly it is far easier to grow them hydroponically.

Using the new HYDRO-TANK

This 60 × 60 cm (24 × 24 in) tray (height = 8 cm (3 in)) has been fitted with a 1 litre (quart) installable S tank, since the seedlings require a constant low water-level. This store lasts for at least 4-5 days, sometimes even longer as the plants get older. The above picture shows the seedlings two weeks after sowing.

water-level of 4-5mm (about ¼ in). I also grew 4 normal cucumbers in a pair of (6/6cm) (2½ in) pots, strawberries and 5 Geraniums, which have long since started to flower. Then I also had two window boxes with fitted tanks, in which I grew Sweet Peas. These climbed up some string which I had drawn from a very convenient horizontal ledge on the edge of the roof of our greenhouse.

As for the expanded clay granules: I found that the finest grain size 0.4mm promoted fastest germination but because the granules were more closely packed together, the growth rate was slower than seedlings growing in pots filled with grain size 4-8mm (¼ - ⅜ in), which permitted better aeration. Size 8-12mm (⅜ - ½ in) granules were used for large seeds such as peas and beans.

Propagation —

If after 10-12 days the plant looks well or has even produced a new shoot, you may remove the bag from time to time to start acclimatizing it. Later you can remove the bag totally.

It is not always easy to classify a cutting because some plants can be propagated in various different ways. Take *Philodendron* as an example. Apart from the fact that you can easily grow them from seeds, which you can buy in special plant shops, the growing points also make excellent cuttings. These will strike all the more readily if you leave a few aerial roots attached to the stem, which you then direct into a separate container of water. Also add a pinch of LEWATIT HD5 to this water. The aerial roots will then provide the cutting with nourishment until its root system, etc., develops.

In the case of Philodendrons, Dieffenbachiae and tree-like plants — prime examples being the very popular Dracaenas and Yuccas — you can take as many **cane cuttings** as you like, by cutting up the trunks into pieces, each being a few centimetres (several inches) in length. They strike easily —

This Wax Plant turned out to be a stem cutting which had struck root at the top.

The natural direction of the leaf growth made it difficult to plant the cutting upside down.

especially in the case of those which prefer warmer temperatures — if you can provide a bottom heat of 25-30°C (77-87°F), but not more!

Air layering is a special form of propagation. This can be carried out at the terminal bud of the growing points which have become too high, especially in the case of Rubber Trees. Unfortunately this process is not always correctly described. The cut is made half-way through the stem, just below the 3rd or 4th leaf joint, so that roots can form and the whole section be

removed later. This cut must be horizontal and not diagonal. Once you used to jam a flat stone between the parts but today you can use a bit of aluminium foil, which is perfectly adequate and does not push away the top part of the stem, which bears the leaves. Such displacement cannot always be avoided if the cut is diagonal and then wedged. *Sphagnum Moss* (the growing medium for orchids) is still the best for wrapping up the cut — if not available, use turf but not sedge peat.

Leafcuttings are another special

Special care had to be taken that no leaves were bent or buried when the aggregate was added.

The cutting is now ready to continue growing. The white spots on the leaves are typical for this plant.

Propagation —

means of propagation. These develop a callus and strike from a leaf stem. This cutting is, as expected, short and depending on the plant may be only a few centimetres (several inches) long. I shall deal with the rolled up leaf of the Rubber Tree first, which is an exception to other leaf cuttings. Here the leaf stem is not shortened and in addition it must have a terminal bud (an 'eye') so that not only roots may develop but also a new plant growth from the 'eye'.

Otherwise, apart from the single leaf continuing to live from its own roots, nothing will happen. True leaf cuttings can be taken from *Peperomiae* and Begonias

Left, a three-leaved bulblet. There is a second flower emerging on the main bulb; right, above the tip of the water-level indicator you can see the main flower stem.

but the most suitable plants grown hydroponically are the *Gesneriaceae* — especially the African Violet. It is clear from the picture opposite how this is done. My two oldest hydroponically grown plants are living proof of such leaf cuttings – especially my show piece from 1963 (see page 65). The leaves shown oposite come from the latter's ''twin'' and you can clearly see the first roots developing from the bottoms of the stems. After an initial attempt at flowering last year, these leaves have now developed into a superb specimen; a new 'twin' which is magnificent and in no way inferior to its mother plant. The producing of **offsets** is a form of vegetative reproduction that is very common among Bromeliads, Clivias and several other kinds of house-plants. If however these are removed too early you will normally find that when they mature they will not flower very successfully.

A perfect example is the *Vriesea splendens*, also called Flaming Sword (see page 68).

Right, three leaves taken from the second of the two African Violets shown on page 65. They are struck through the holes in the polythene covering the jar, and are immersed in the water containing a few LEWATIT HD5 granules. These leaf cuttings do not require nodes for striking and the new roots are growing from the cutting point.

Propagation —

The bulblet's leaf had already grown almost too large.

Part of the inner pot had to be cut away in order to free the bulblet.

The **plantlets** that form at the end of the inflorescences of *Chlorophytum* (The Spider Plant) previously discussed, are also examples of vegetative reproduction, as are the runners of some Ferns such as *Nephrolepsis*, the Ladder Fern, which are very easy to propagate. "Teddy Junior" is a very popular cultivar of the latter type and on page 61 there is a superb specimen of this plant. Since the propagation of cacti and other succulents and its ease and success has already been discussed in the chapter titled "Our selection of plants" (page 72ff), all that still remains to be covered here are **bulbs**.

The great advantages of growing flowering bulbs in hydroponics were listed when we were dealing with these plants earlier. One such example was the ease with which bulbs reproduce. It is also very simple to remove the bulblets and to grow a new plant — especially in the case of Amaryllis, *Hippeastrum*. The pot used should always be large enough to afford several years' growth. The first flower stem usually appears after 2-3 years. Until then the plant has to be grown all year long, i.e., the foliage must not be removed at the end of the summer and the plant must remain indoors for the

Separate the bulblet from its mother with a sharp knife.

The process has been successfully completed and the bulblet does indeed have fully formed roots.

winter, ignoring the resting period.

The results from vegetative reproduction are excellent. Good examples are the Amaryllises known as *Crinum, Hymenocallis* (Cape Lily), *Sprekelia* (Aztec Lily), *Vallota* (Scarborough Lily) which is very popular at the moment and another member of the Lily family, *Veltheimia*.

Removal of the baby bulb should only take place when it has reached full maturity, after the flower has finished blooming.

When the new plant is put into its pot, the point of which the bulblet was cut should face upwards and remain uncovered so that it can dry out.

Plant protection — a must

When my first book on hydroponics appeared in 1967, this chapter bore the title "Plant protection — only incidental". In it I stressed the enormous difference between traditional cultivation of plants in soil, in which one finds all kinds of harmful organisms, and hydroponics, which one could call "chemically pure". At that time the as yet still small circle of staunch hydroponicists really did have reason to be convinced that, on the whole, their hydroponically grown plants were as good as safe from fungal and bacterial disease and from most pests. These plants were grown in stone chippings and the nutrient solution required frequent changing, for hydroponics was still at an early stage of development — although, I hasten to add, this method still provides "optimal conditions" then, as now. But even then I pointed out that nothing can be perfect and infections in the part of the plant above-ground cannot be ruled out, all the more when one has to take into account that infection might be brought in from outside or transmitted some other way.

If in those days, when hydroponicists were mostly a dedicated few, yet mistakes were still made, then today, when hydroponics has been widely popularized, the spread in demand must also have resulted in new dangers.

'Optimal care' is supposed to ensure that the plant is so healthy it can resist all infection of its own accord.

But this is in many ways an over-simplification. Before a plant can be brought to such a state it would already have undergone many risks. For example, say that in spite of exemplary hygiene in the hydroponic nurseries a plant was unfortunately infected by an outside source — for instance

Plant lice not only attack the young shoots and leaves of the Hibiscus but also the buds and flowers. The usual cause of infection is too warm a position in the winter and insufficient humidity. If there is also a lack of light then the flower buds will fall off.

Plant protection — a must

with red spider mites, thrips or one of the many flies. This would then spread rapidly, promoted by the fact that a large number of plants will inevitably be of the same type. A buyer might unknowingly buy such an infected plant and put his other plants at risk. Infection at home would be promoted by any of his own cultural faults, which would mean his plants are not strong enough to resist infection.

Lasting protection is gained not from short-term measures such as spraying, but from meticulous general care.

So, do not just ascertain what the infection actually is, but check if all the necessary conditions for optimal growth are fulfilled for each plant — sufficient light and warmth, the correct placing and above all, sufficient nutrition and the right nutrient solution level — preferably a bit lower than too high.
I have already discussed what aids are available to check these conditions, from the light meter and MERCKOQUANT strips, to measuring the water-level with an old-fashioned dipstick instead of relying on a water-level indicator that may be faulty.

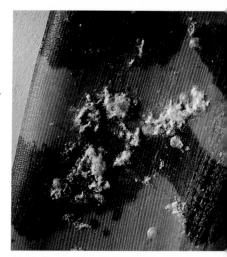

Mealy Bug on the underside of a *Vrieseae splendens* leaf. The white cottony fluff is a typical symptom of infection.

Scale on the underside of a fern frond. It is best to use a systemic insecticide to destroy these pests which have very strong shells.

Plant protection — a must

The winter is the most critical period for hydroponically grown plants which do not require a resting period at low temperatures of 10-15°C (50-59°F) and an almost total withholding of nutrient solution. For these a dry and over-warm atmosphere is just as dangerous as if they were in a cold room, standing in too high a level of nutrient solution and consequently had "cold feet". In the latter case the result would be rotting roots and serious weakening of the plant ranging from a general bad condition to death. In the former rankness and a susceptibility to pests and infection are inevitable.

The pests shown here in color do not just attack the plants depicted but, of course, many others too.

This means that, for example, scale insects, thrips or the red spider mite which is so feared not without justification, are just as likely to attack Dracaenae, Philodendrons, cacti and other succulents. Similarly plant lice and mealy bug can be found on many other plants. The mealy bugs excrete a substance known as "honey dew"; a sticky, sweet liquid on which a black fungus called Sooty Mould may appear which leaves a black coating. Both are harmless and can be removed from plants and furniture without a problem, simply just by washing with luke-warm water.

*But beware! Honey dew is a danger signal indicating heavier larvae infection. Large plants (e.g., **Ficus benjamina, Schefflera** should be washed down with lukewarm water in the bath (first cover the top of the hydroponic container with polythene) before spraying with insecticide.*

Thrips has unfortunately now become quite common in hydroponic nurseries and from there it may spread into your home. It is easy to recognize by its silvery sheen as on a Rubber Tree leaf.

Plant protection — a must

Red spider mites can hardly be seen with the naked eye. Left, an uninfected leaf; right, an *Aphelandra* leaf which appears reddish as a result of infestation.

Their pernicious effect is initially indicated by this swelling.

There are of course a number of insecticides available to combat the above named pests, but not all of them are equally effective or safe for all plants. Here you have to be especially careful with different plants that are grown together. Using an aerosol can damage the overall health of your plant if you fail to keep sufficient distance from the plant when you spray it — the active ingredient causes severe chill and leaf damage. The minimum distance to be kept from the plant is therefore 30cm (12in). The preparation

SYSTEMSCHUTZ D-HYDRO was specially developed for hydroponics by WACKER CHEMICALS in Munich and is particularly excellent for all plant lice. Its effect on other sap-sucking pests is good but slower. It is applied internally, by adding it to the nutrient solution, a major innovation. It does not matter what kind of nutrient solution is being used. You must, however, follow the instructions carefully.

The red spider mite is not an insect but belongs to the family

119

Plant protection — a must

Root rot can attack Amaryllis and other bulbs. In the picture on the left you can clearly recognize the red patches that are a sign of infection. Later the tissue of the flower stem will be attacked and destroyed, causing its collapse. Infected plants should be eradicated.

Mildew infection on a *Elatior* Begonia. This is really the beginning of the end; mildew is the precursor of the fatal **Stengel-Bakteriose**.

of arachnids and may therefore not always respond to the usual insecticides.

Occasionally people have considered importing the red spider parasite Phytoseuilius to combat the problem "naturally" but unfortunately this is out of the question for domestic use and in hydroponics. A systematic remedy for the red spider mite is, however,

Plant protection — a must

desperately needed, for this pest is the arch-enemy of hydroponicists and horticulturists alike. Until one is found, we shall have to make do with the various aerosols available, even if these are not always suitable.

Such sprays cannot possibly be used for fungi infections such as root rot which not only attacks Amaryllis *Hippeastrum)* but other bulbs too which are of interest in hydroponics. Healthy bulbs will not usually be attacked unless you bring in the fungus *Stagonospora* from an outside source, by buying an infected plant — it may be a *Crinum, Sprekelia* or *Vallota*. I must say, experts blame the recent increase in this fungus infection on the mass breeding of plants in nurseries, where infection will spread all the more rapidly. Plants infected are considered incurable. The same applies to *Elatior* — Begonias. Once infected with mildew death is inevitable, irrespective of whether they are grown in soil or hydroponically.

There is no cure. Your only option is to eradicate the plant immediately.

Finally we come to Springtails which belong to the oldest family of insects. Their predilection for plants grown hydroponically is one of the most amazing modern examples of adaptation. When containers with nutrient solution did not exist, they lived — and some still do today — in flower pots filled with turfy soil which had been overwatered, and also in compost heaps. The damage they do is relatively minor and you do not need chemical preparations such as NEMAPHOS-EMULSION to get rid of them. All that is required is a few drops of a good dish-washing liquid which simply reduces the surface tension of the nutrient solution, thereby effectively killing all Springtails.

Infection by **Springtail** also known as white worm, (natural size 1-3 mm) are relatively harmless and easy to combat.

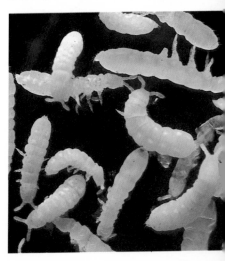

The worst cultural faults

These mistakes are all the small and large errors and oversights which can happen even to the most careful and knowledgeable of hydroponicists. They can, however, have the most unexpected effects on your plants and the causes may be very difficult to trace.

The damage done may be attributable to various causes, one of which may actually be the real culprit.

Some of the worst mistakes in general care are the result of forgetfulness. If there is nothing to help remind you to water your plants, no summer's heat, no note book, no aid to jog your memory, then even the rarest of the rare may occur — the leaves of your plant may droop and the buds fall off as a result of insufficient moisture. Even if the pot is stood in warmed water, this remedy may not be able to halt the progress of the damage.

The best solution is to keep a diary. This is a lesson I also had to learn.

And of course, to be on the safe side it is always best to check the plants once more than should be strictly necessary. Tap the water-level indicator, observe the float and in the case of an emergency resort to the old method of measuring the water-level with a dipstick — after all, once there was no other method and it was successfully used for a long time.

Although they do have their advantages, leaf polishes can only be used for hard-leaved plants and even then not unless they are sprayed onto the top surface of the leaf.

Treating the underside blocks up pores and damages the plant by interfering with its breathing apparatus.

Leaf fall in the early spring means this *Schefflera* has had too low a winter temperature (below 12°C 54°F). It can also result in the sudden loss of all its foliage.

The worst cultural faults

Milk, beer or even oil are strictly forbidden for use as polishes. It is best to clean large, firm leaves with absorbent cotton balls dipped in lukewarm water. But now we are again on the familiar subject of general plant-care.

Light, warmth and water-level are the three main factors for a plant's well-being. These must be kept under constant observation, bearing in mind their inter-dependence.

Holidays are potentially the most dangerous times for all plants, for the owners simply forget to make special provisions in their absence and the plant's most basic requirements are often not met.

Returning to the subject of transferring plants to hydroponics, it is imperative that this is completed at least 8 weeks before going on holiday. Only then can you tell if your plant has already overcome the 'risk' and will be able to take the minor restrictions imposed if you are away for a while. Only then will there be no major setbacks. For when you are on holiday — in the case of small containers with a low nutrient solution capacity, remove the pot and place into flat trays which will serve as 'reservoirs'.

This *Aglaonema* hybrid "Silverking" was a healthy, beautiful Christmas present. One and a half years later it was a very different sight — see below. Various cultural errors were to blame.

The worst cultural faults

The level of the water will depend on the size of the plants, temperature and light conditions. The best caretaker for your plants, in your absence, is the HYDRO-TANK, but even its advantages come to nought if the blinds are down for weeks on end.

Some important advice: Never put house-plants into a newly painted or decorated room. The fumes from the paints and adhesives (also used for laying carpets, etc.) can be fatal for plants. Wait at least 2 weeks before replacing them.

And do remember — your plants still need looking after properly even in the excitement and confusion that arises when workmen are in the house or when you are in the process of moving. A totally irresponsible advertisement on the other hand boasts that hydroponically grown plants "look after themselves". This is simply not true. If you want to have long-term enjoyment from your plants then you must meet their requirements.

And if someone tells you that hydroponics is 'boring' because "there is nothing for you to do", then he is totally on the wrong track. Even if hydroponically grown plants live in expanded clay granules, they still need people to look after them and, who knows, even to give them a bit of love.

A few technical expressions

As I have said before, this book is for the layman. But in other books on the subject you may well come across terms which will present difficulties; accessories may be recommended which are either too specialized or now out-dated, and although not available in the shops, these may be a source of confusion for the reader.

To give a few examples:

Pumice-stone gravel — a growing medium used in the early days of hydroponics; only for special purposes.

Biolaston, "Potsdam aggregate" — the left-overs of man-made bristles from brush factories.

Silicon-mica — fine, sand-like expanded clay granules recently recommended for nursery care. Beware, it disrupts capillary attraction.

Expanded Slate — noteworthy alternative to expanded clay granules. Not yet on sale.

Conductivity Meter — used to measure the salt content of the nutrient solution in garden centers.

Perlite — a volcanic stone made porous by heat treatment; propagation aggregate used in nurseries.

"Plantanova" — special vases made of tinted glass with a shallow fitted tray. Used in early hydroponics, now obsolete.

Rockwool — propagation medium. Serious risk of excessive water retention — often the reason why bought plants die. Same dangers as Grodan.

Temik — often used to protect plants by greenhouse growers. Highly poisonous substance; not to be used at home.

Vermiculite — a so-called secondary mineral, once highly esteemed as a complete aggregate, but in the long run it would stick together. Nowadays mainly used as a supplement to the growing medium.

Index

The plants mentioned in the chapter headed 'Our selection of plants' pp 52–87 are only mentioned here in part; the same applies to the technical terms on page 124. In both cases reference is easy. Bold page numbers indicate either an illustration or a main topic.

Index

Index